ːGE

THE UNIVERSITY OF
WINCHESTER

# GYMNASTICS 7-11:

## A SESSION-BY-SESSION APPROACH TO KEY STAGE 2

# ACKNOWLEDGMENTS

*Photographs*:  Les Cross, Brighton Polytechnic
*The children*:  Bevendean Primary School, Brighton
*Illustrations*:  Marilyn Amos

# GYMNASTICS 7-11:
## A SESSION-BY-SESSION APPROACH TO KEY STAGE 2

M.E. CARROLL

AND

H.K. MANNERS
*Brighton Polytechnic*

The Falmer Press
*(A member of the Taylor & Francis Group)*
LONDON, NEW YORK & PHILADELPHIA

| UK | The Falmer Press, 4 John St, London WC1N 2ET |
| USA | The Falmer Press, Taylor & Francis Inc., 1900 Frost Road, Suite 101, Bristol, PA 19007 |

---

First published in 1991
Reprinted in 1992

**British Library Cataloguing in Publication Data available on request**

ISBN 0 75070 002 5

Jacket design by Caroline Archer

Typeset in 10/11 pt Times
by Graphicraft Typesetters Ltd. Hong Kong.
Printed and bound in Hong Kong

# CONTENTS

# PREFACE

This teachers' workbook is a re-designed Key Stage 2 (Years 3–6) version of the original *Gymnastics 7–11* by M.E. Carroll and D.R. Garner first published in 1984 and reprinted several times since.

It is the second volume of a two volume workbook — Volume I being a newly written workbook for Years R-2 (Key Stage 1) by H.K. Manners and M.E. Carroll, *Movement Leading to Gymnastics 4–7: A Session-by-Session Approach to Key Stage 1*, also published by Falmer Press.

The need for Volume I became self evident once the original *Gymnastics 7–11* was launched. Teachers of the younger children asked for the same kind of *session by session* approach, which would meet their own particular needs, and which would also be consistent with likely developments in respect of the National Curriculum.

Both volumes follow a similar format and approach and are designed to be a progressively developing programme of work from Year R — Year 6 (Key Stages 1 and 2).

M.E. Carroll
H.K. Manners
*Brighton Polytechnic*
April 1991

# INTRODUCTION: KEY STAGE 2

This programme is designed to promote the development of more stylised gymnastic movement which leads on from the 'Movement Education' approach in Key Stage 1.

Children in the later primary years of schooling are becoming capable of developing and performing carefully controlled movements and movement phrases which are pleasing both to watch and perform and which are skilful in their execution.

Some of the work may appear to repeat that which was asked of the younger children (in Key Stage 1) — but the focus is now different. The children should be concentrating more particularly on correctness, on control and on the beauty of their movements. It is *not* a backward step if this focus is emphasized.

However, it is not intended that each of the early sessions of Year 3 must be taught if teachers feel that their children have already experienced this work.

**What is Involved in Gymnastics**

Definitions are often difficult and imprecise. A definition of gymnastics is not necessarily helpful — yet it is necessary to know what characterizes the work. It would seem that whatever form of gymnastics is evident (Olympic, rhythmic, educational, sports acrobatics, vaulting and agility) certain kinds of attributes give the work its name gymnastics. It has several components worth examining.

**Physical component**
This includes:
(i)  A degree of strength sufficient for the work to be performed safely — mainly jump/push/flexion/extension strength. If these

1

are not improved then certain aspects will always be beyond the child.
(ii) A degree of flexibility sufficient to enable the safe execution of many aspects — mainly shoulder, hip, ankle flexibility.

**Skill component** (with or without apparatus)
This includes running, jumping and landing, balance, rotation, springs, swings, supports, flight, linkage.

**Aesthetic component**
A concern
(i)  for the shape and line of the action where the children concentrate on the beauty of their movements;
(ii) for the kinaesthetic satisfaction of having got it just right.

**Creative component**
True creativity shown by some international gymnasts is reflected in novel movements derived from a structured and disciplined training. At a lower level, however, the children can be seen to produce/create a series of movements which may be novel to themselves.

**Psychological component**
This includes:
(i)  A degree of courage.
(ii) A degree of perseverance.

**Cognitive component**
An understanding of how the body moves — rotation, centre of gravity, force etc.

If then these factors need to be present for the activity to be called *gymnastics*, and if the work is to happen in school, then a teaching approach must be adopted which will, on the one hand, generate the development of these essential characteristics and, on the other, will also be a relevant educational experience. Children should therefore be able to demonstrate bodily skill on the floor, on apparatus, and with a partner, because this is the aim of the work. How the teacher achieves such an aim is the next stage of the argument.

It is here that the differing needs of the developing child must be considered. The young infant (in school) is using the 'gymnastic' environment to explore a range of movement options — and this exploration may be clumsy and unrefined. The role of the teacher at this stage is to intervene to make the children *conscious* of what they are doing, so that they are both *moving* and *knowing*. As the children become more mature the teacher seeks to develop more stylized, skilled bodily action — which has a clearer resemblance to recognized gymnastic forms.

By the end of the later primary years, children should be capable of demonstrating skilled and harmonious body action, showing discrimination in their selection of work to practise and perform.

If gymnastics is about bodily skill (as it undoubtedly is), and if we want our children to be proficient in using skilled body movement in answer to various kinds of tasks, the method adopted must operate fully along the methodological continuum of open-ended (process) — closed (product). It makes sense to do this since some activities require direct teaching, whereas others lend themselves to a more experimental approach. Sometimes the teacher will set tasks which tightly constrain what the children may do (*e.g.* learning to take weight safely on hands — a handstand). At other times, children may need to demonstrate understanding of a movement concept in their performance and so the task will be of a different order (*e.g.* devise a sequence of turns about the three axes of the body). There are also many other stages in between which are more or less constraining. All of these stages feature in this workbook in a structured progressive form. Different kinds of tasks are given which demand different kinds of response from the children. The whole programme has an inbuilt development of skill learning, movement understanding, and composing.

**The Approach**   In order to facilitate the ordering of subject matter, and its presentation to children, the whole programme is written in *session* format. The sessions are planned so that they develop the material of gymnastics in different forms, in order to ensure progression of skill, of movement understanding and of individual response to movement tasks.

The *content* selected highlights the essential characteristics of gymnastics and reflects the belief that gymnastics is chiefly concerned with bodily skill. It is classified into **units of work** (often called 'Themes' in other texts) aspects of which form the focus of a series of sessions. Each session will, in turn, have its own specific emphasis:

*e.g.* UNIT         : ROTATION
      EMPHASIS : Turning into and out of balance.

The units are different in the two major age phases (4–7 and 7–11) in order to facilitate the development through from 4–11 as already indicated.

All units are *action* focussed (*i.e.* they focus on *what* the body can do) and other qualitative and spatial aspects are used as a means of developing the action focus (see *Achieving Variety*). In the 7–11 phase, Partner Work is considered as a unit, but it always relates to an action context.

*Teaching method* is the key to successful development of the content. Throughout the programme it is task-oriented and the tasks are of different kinds. They may be of a problem-solving nature, ask for repetitive practice, relate directly to learning a specific skill, or encourage experimentation.

Tasks become increasingly demanding as the programme progresses. They call for:

(i)     greater competence in basic skills;
(ii)    a greater vocabulary of movements;
(iii)   greater awareness of body line;
(iv)    increased ability to show variety in the work;
(v)     greater fluency in linking movements;
(vi)    increased ability to refine and compose movement sequences;
(vii)   an ability to work skilfully and cooperatively with a partner;
(viii)  greater understanding of how the body moves.

Where tasks relate to teaching specific skills, reference should be made to the **Specific Skills Guide**, in conjunction with the session plan. Specific skills are incorporated in three ways:

(i)    as skills in their own right;
(ii)   as required movements within unit-focussed tasks;
(iii)  as a basis for children's own interpretation of some tasks.

Examples of these can be found throughout the book.
*Sessions* are also of different kinds. They each begin with some form of WARM UP and BODY PREPARATION (see **Physiological Guide**) but then are developed as appropriate to the particular stage of learning. Thus some sessions may then move into entirely floor-based activity, whilst others may combine floor work and apparatus work. Others may develop work on large apparatus arrangements, or just on mats. The variety is intentional and is necessary if the work is to develop systematically. Session format is as follows:

| Content | Teaching points |
|---|---|
| The task which is given to the children | The emphases needed for ensuring satisfactory response to the work and/or notes to the teacher. |

If time allows, a FINAL ACTIVITY, may conclude each session. Normally this should be a strengthening activity (see **Physiological Guide**), followed by a calming activity (see also *Introduction to Key Stage 1*) — e.g. standing quietly and well before moving calmly out of the hall. (NB. always include a calming activity.) Ideas for strengthening activities are included at the end of the **Physiological Guide**.

Some sessions have many tasks whilst others have relatively few. At times, tasks may be general, and relate to all groups of children, whilst at other times the task set may be for a specific group. This again is an intentional feature of the whole programme. It is most important, however, that teachers should feel they are able to repeat sessions. IN FACT SOME SESSIONS WILL NEED TO BE REPEATED.

At the end of each term there is an assessment and revision section which indicates what it is hoped the children will have learnt.

It is most important that this whole programme of gymnastics is seen as a progressive learning package. Whilst it is recognized that when first introducing it into a school it may be necessary for older children to begin at the earlier stages if their experience is limited, in time there will only be a structured development of gymnastics throughout the school if everyone works with the plan. *It is only when a school decides to use such a plan, AND works with it over a number of years, that real progress will be seen in the teaching of gymnastics.*

## Units

The units are:
    (i)   Travelling
    (ii)  Balance
    (iii) Rotation
    (iv) Springing and Landing, and
    (v)  (though different) Partner work.

Units are revisited several times during the sessions so that skills *and* concepts may develop progressively. This is a most important feature of the programme.

### (i)   Travelling

This is a basic unit in gymnastics (and is sometimes seen as 'Locomotion') which seeks to explore:
(a) Different methods of travelling; running, jumping, rolling etc.;
(b) Different body parts for travelling: feet, hands and feet, combinations of parts etc.;
    … across the floor, on mats and low apparatus, on large apparatus.

### (ii)   Balance

Balance is important in gymnastics because as in all movement, it is constantly lost and regained in order for the body to change position. Generally speaking 'balance' can be defined as any body position where the centre of gravity lies within the base of support. Obviously the wider the base of support, the more stable the position. Ideally the feeling should be one of being *perched* not resting. The children should fully grasp the concept of balance and appreciate that the smaller the base of support the more difficult it is to maintain balance and the further away the Centre of Gravity is from the base, once again the more unstable the balance. Children need to experience 'on balance' positions using different parts of the body as the base of support. Additionally they must experience moving into balance and moving out of balance (consciously knowing when they are 'in balance' and 'off balance').

### (iii)   Rotation

Rotation is concerned with turning and twisting of the body. Many turning and twisting actions will naturally have been experienced in work centred on *Travelling*, but are now further developed. Turning actions occur around the three main axes of the body:

    longitudinal (up/down)
    medial (through centre of body — back/front)
    lateral (through centre of body — side/side)

Children should experience turning actions around all three axes, using different kinds of action, on different body parts.

Twisting occurs when there is torsion between different parts of the body which when built up can give impetus for other actions (recoil effect). Equally twisting can be used to initiate a change of direction in the direction of the twist.

### (iv)  Springing and Landing

As a development of the work in jumping, this unit revises and reinforces key points related generally to jumping, but moves a stage further to develop actions which spring onto and from the hands (in combination with other springing actions). Children will experience springing onto and from the floor and the apparatus using specific springing skills, and use these skills in movement sequences. It is important that children are sufficiently strong in the arms for undertaking this work. They must be safe and competent in terms of bodily control, particularly when receiving weight from a height.

### (v)  Partner Work

This unit capitalizes on the fact that children enjoy working together. It should not be thought of however, as merely a means of repeating individual tasks with another person. The following checklist of questions may be used to see if the work is being developed effectively:

(a)  Is there INTERDEPENDENCE between the two children?
(b)  Do the children adapt, modify, adjust their own movements to meet the demands of the partner task?
(c)  Are the children observing accurately the work of their partner in readiness for their part?
(d)  Are the children strong/controlled enough to take all or part of their partner's weight?
(e)  Is the *quality* of the work still good?

The work centres first on non-contact partner activity then on simple contact activity. Each lesson or series of lessons has a specific movement focus (*e.g.* it may relate to *Balance* or *Rotation*).

**Achieving Variety**    It is possible to examine movement as follows:
Asking:

| | | |
|---|---|---|
| (i) | WHAT? | Actions are being done (Jumping, Running, Wheeling etc.) |
| | | Body parts are being used (Hands, Feet, Knees etc.) |
| | | Body shape is being adopted (Tucked, elongated, spread etc.) |
| (ii) | HOW? | Fast/slow: Leading into accelerating/ decelerating |
| | | Vigorous/Light: Strong tension/light tension |

(iii) WHERE?     On spot/generally in space
                 Levels: (high, low)
                 Directions: (forward, backward, sideways,
                 upwards etc.)
                 Pathways (curved, zig-zagged, straight etc.)

(iv) WITH WHOM?  A Partner
                 Two others
                 Alone

THUS to achieve variety ask the children to repeat previous movements with a named change, related to what?, how?, where?, or with whom?

*E.g. Initial task:* Develop a pattern of 3 jumps which travel
*Variations:* (i)   Emphasize clear leg positions (together, apart, bent/straight) = WHAT? variation.
          (ii)  The second jump must show a distinct change of body shape = WHAT? variation.
          (iii) The jumps must increase in height = HOW? variation.
          (iv)  The first two must be clearly on the spot and the final jump moves to another place = SPACE/WHERE? variation.
          (v)   Make the jumps follow a zig-zag pathway and one jump must include a *turn* = WHERE?, variation + WHAT?
          (vi)  Using a bench find a way of sharing your pattern with a partner = WITH WHOM? variation.

Examples as this can be found throughout the programme.

**Skill**  As stated in the *Introduction*, gymnastics *is bodily* skill.
The intention of gymnastics is bodily action — skilled bodily action.

Thus the children need to learn how to become skilled movers. Then they will have more options open to them for creating their own movement phrases — and these will be more pleasing to them.

Throughout this section, therefore, skilled body management is demanded at two levels.

(1) At a general level where children develop general action competence.

    *e.g.* UNIT            : TRAVELLING
           General Actions : Rolling
                             Jumping
                             Wheeling etc.

(2) Then at a more specific level where children develop competence in named specific skills.

```
e.g.  UNIT              : TRAVELLING
      General Actions  : Rolling
      Specific skill   : Forward Roll.
```

In order for this to happen, specific skills are introduced at particular points in the programme — usually to the whole class — but at an introductory level.

This enables the whole class to learn the basics of the skill ACCURATELY and SAFELY. Then, since children will be at different levels of ability, more specific practice of skills in their own right is located in the group activity part of a session.

Teachers may include a skill practice group at any stage if they feel the children will benefit. In this way children who need more help can be encouraged to improve, and those who have learnt the skill can be using the skill in a more open-ended task.

The **Specific Skills Guide** gives precise details of each of the basic skills.

**Task Cards**  These are effective and interesting for the development of gymnastics.

In the sessions where different groups have different tasks it is helpful if these are reproduced as separate task cards. The children can then carry out the tasks independently of the teacher.

Suggestions for using cards are included where appropriate through the programme.

**Apparatus**  This workbook ideally requires the following apparatus for a class of 30; this ensures maximum activity. However, the programme can still be followed with less apparatus by increasing the number of children in each group or by using alternative pieces of apparatus, *e.g.* stage blocks.

6 Benches
8 Mats, 6' × 4'
1 Springboard (Reuther, if possible) (NB. check LEA guidelines)
4 10' Planks
2 Stools/Stacking Tables
1 Bar Box
1 Climbing frame
2 Movement/Agility Tables.

## Key

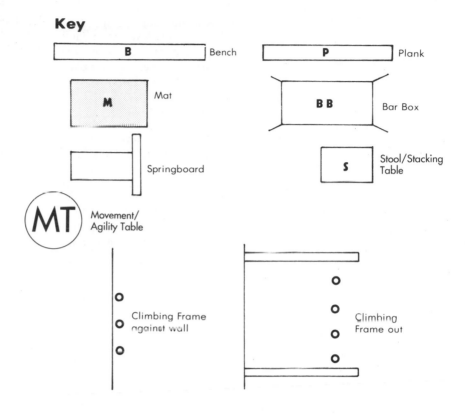

B — Bench

P — Plank

M — Mat

BB — Bar Box

— Springboard

S — Stool/Stacking Table

MT — Movement/Agility Table

Climbing Frame against wall

Climbing Frame out

**Safety**   The safety of the children must be uppermost in the teacher's mind at all times. Accidents do occur, but most can be avoided if the teacher is vigilant and careful.

(i) **The Hall**
   A large uninterrupted floor area is the most important aid to any physical education lesson, and schools should ensure that a sufficient working area is provided. In most schools the hall is a multi-use area, catering not only for physical education but also music, drama, school lunches, and assemblies. A great amount of thought is needed to arrange the storage in the most economical way. The following points need to be remembered:
   (a) Leave a large, free area of regular shape.
   (b) Allow free access to all cupboards.
   (c) Position apparatus so that it is easily moved into position by the children. Note: Apparatus which is difficult to get out is often not used.
   (d) If the hall is used as a corridor, leave sufficient space for a direct route so that the classes are not disturbed.
   (e) Check that the floor of the hall is clean, splinter-proof and non-slippery.

(ii) **Clothing**
   (a) Pupils should change into appropriate clothing for gymnastic lessons. This clothing should allow freedom of movement on

the floor and apparatus. Where the floor is suitable children should work with bare feet. Jewellery should not be worn; this can be potentially dangerous to the wearer as well as others.

(b) The teacher should also, of course, wear suitable clothing and safe footwear.

(iii) **The Apparatus**

(a) It is the responsibility of the teacher to make sure that the apparatus is handled and used correctly and is safe to use.

(b) Portable and fixed apparatus should be examined once a year by a gymnastic contractor.

(c) **No child** should use the apparatus unless a member of staff is present.

(d) Before the apparatus is used, the teacher should:
Check the positioning of the apparatus before it is used.
Check the fixing of the apparatus.
Make sure that the height of the apparatus is suitable for the size and ability of the pupil.
Train the children to handle the apparatus safely and efficiently.

(e) Improvised apparatus **should not be allowed**.

(f) The following activities **should not be permitted**:
Dive forward rolls over apparatus, including benches and over human obstacles.
Competitive racing and chasing games on apparatus, 'pirates'.
Activities involving the use of trampettes.

(g) Carrying and erecting apparatus. There is such a variety of apparatus in use through the country that it is very difficult to give specific advice. However, assuming that children are expected to get out and put away apparatus, a few general rules can be observed by children.
Always look where you are going (*e.g.* if the children are carrying a plank or bench they should ideally all be facing the direction in which they are moving).
Apparatus should never be lifted over other children.
Apparatus should always be lowered gently to prevent damage to the floor, the apparatus and children's feet.
Apparatus, including mats, should never be dragged along the floor.
Develop a system which is adopted by all classes in the school in terms of carrying and storage. This will generate efficiency as the children progress through the school.

(h) Positioning of apparatus. The teacher should bear the following points in mind when planning the apparatus arrangement:
A clear space should be left around apparatus.
It should never be positioned so that children, when jumping, can stumble into an obstruction.

(i) Supervision of apparatus work.
The corner of the hall or gymnasium may be the most suitable place to stand so that all work can be seen. The

teacher should try not to stand facing away from the class even when assisting a pupil.

If a teacher has to leave the hall or gymnasium in an extreme emergency pupils should be ordered off the apparatus and even out of the hall altogether.

Different teachers will naturally be working at different stages of the programme with their classes. They may or may not require apparatus. Thus the practice of apparatus being left out for several classes is not relevant. If children are taught how to assemble all pieces efficiently and with control, the process of handling will be quite simple, whatever arrangement is planned. Apparatus should be easily accessible round the perimeter of the hall not left in the store room which causes congestion and difficulties.

# THE SESSION-BY-SESSION APPROACH TO KEY STAGE 2

# YEAR 3

**Autumn Term:** **TRAVELLING**
**Session 1:** **On feet**

| | Content | Teaching points |
|---|---|---|
| **Warm up** | 1 Soft running in and out of whole class. | 1 Attention to spacing. Good carriage of body. (See *Specific Skills Guide* — Running.) |
| **Body preparation** | 1 Bouncing on spot (feet together) getting higher and higher. | 1 Full extension through legs. Help from arms in lifting. Neck relaxed (See *Specific Skills Guide* — Jumping.) |
| | 2 a) Sitting, ankle bending and stretching<br>b) Standing, feet astride — hip circling slowly<br>c) Sitting, cross-legged, gently press head on floor between knees. | 2 Ensure full mobility. |
| **Floor activities** | 1 Keeping away from others, show different ways of travelling on feet. | 1 Articulate to class the range of activities that the children show. |
| | 2 Repeat, travelling less distance, concentrating on foot stretching in all activities. | 2 Prepare feet for next action — stretch and use feet precisely. |
| | 3 Isolate bouncing on the spot. | 3 Stretched ankles and legs. Strong extension in knees. (See *Specific Skills Guide* — Jumping.) |
| | 4 Repeat on the move for *just a few* jumps. | 4 Good body carriage *plus* Teaching Points as in 3. |

| Content | Teaching points |
|---|---|
| **Content** | **Teaching points** |
| 5 Develop a pattern of *going* and *stopping* with bounces (use direction changes). | 5 Clear and simple — able to be repeated. |
| 6 Practise another jump which is not a bounce. | 6 Enumerate varying possibilities if necessary (*e.g.* leap, hop). |
| 7 Make a pattern to show soft running, bouncing and the jump you have just practised. | 7 Encourage children to make elements short and precise. They must remember it and perfect it. |

**Final activity**   Stand well.

Look for a plumb line from shoulder through hips to knees and ankles.

# YEAR 3

**Autumn Term:** **TRAVELLING**
**Session 2:** **On feet**

| | Content | Teaching points |
|---|---|---|
| **Warm up** | 1 Running softly and jumping generally in space. | 1 Land with bent knees and then spring STRAIGHT UP again. |
| **Body preparation** | 1 Bouncing on spot, increasing in height. | 1 Full stretch in legs. Use arms to help lift. |
| | 2 a) Foot circling<br>b) Lie on side, slowly circle top leg as far as possible. Change sides. | 2 Ensure full mobility. |
| **Floor activities** | 1 Keeping in space, show the different ways of travelling on feet which you practised last time. | 1 Articulate to class the range of activities that the children show. Remind them past experience. |
| | 2 Quick reminder of running, bouncing and jumping. | 2 Good body carriage, stretched legs and feet.<br>*Note*: Do not travel too far |
| **Apparatus activities** | Benches and mats only — or tops of boxes or nesting tables, etc. | |
| | 1 Individually: try some of the ways of travelling using bench, floor and mat. | 1 Remind children of (a) variety possible; (b) possible combinations of floor, bench and mat. |
| | 2 Travel towards the bench using one method, along or across a second method and off using a third method. | 2 Start away from bench. Remind of good leg and ankle extension. Arms help in lift. |

| Content | Teaching points |
|---------|-----------------|
| **Final activity** | Apparatus away.<br>Stand well. |

**Apparatus pattern**

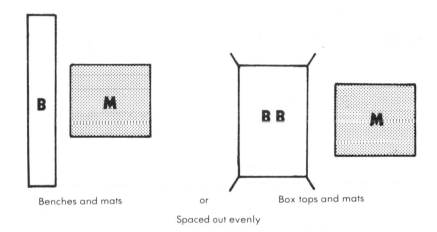

Benches and mats        or        Box tops and mats

Spaced out evenly

# YEAR 3

**Autumn Term:** TRAVELLING
**Session 3:** On feet

|  | Content | Teaching points |
|---|---|---|
| **Warm up** | 1 Soft running in and out of whole class. | 1 Attention to spacing. Good carriage of body. (See *Specific Skills Guide* — Running.) |
|  | 2 Running softly and jumping. | 2 Landing with bent knees and springing STRAIGHT UP again. |
| **Body preparation** | 1 Lie on back. Take legs over head to touch knees on the floor on either side of the head. | 1 Helps trunk mobility. |
|  | 2 Stand up and stretch alternate arms upwards. | 2 Keep trunk still. |
| **Apparatus activities** | Benches and mats as in Session 2. |  |
|  | 1 Practise bounces along the bench. | 1 Precision and control. Head up if possible. |
|  | 2 Skip a few steps on the bench and spring off on to mat (sideways). | 2 As above: bent knees landing to mat and spring up again. |
|  | 3 Run half-way along bench and pause. Spring to floor. | 3 Stretch up on pause ... flex legs and spring — landing as in 2. |
|  | 4 Make up, and repeat, a pattern of travelling on feet (different methods) using the words *on to*, *off*, and *across*, the bench. | 4 Try to encourage quite short patterns which are clear and repeatable. Order need not be as in content. |

|                | **Content**                                                                 | **Teaching points**                                               |
| -------------- | --------------------------------------------------------------------------- | ----------------------------------------------------------------- |
|                | 5 All show your ACROSS movement. Ditto ON TO Ditto OFF.                      | 5 This helps clarify. Ask for good quality in all these actions.  |
|                | 6 Repeat 4.                                                                  |                                                                   |

**Final activity**  With control, in groups, squat jumps round the mat and back to place.

Backs erect.
(A leg strengthening activity.)

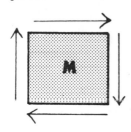

Apparatus away.
Stand well.

# YEAR 3

**Autumn Term:** TRAVELLING
**Session 4:** With jumping (5 basic jumps)

| | Content | Teaching points |
|---|---|---|
| **Warm up** | 1 Soft running, sprint short distance on signal and return to soft running. | 1 Ensure correct leg and arm action for sprinting. Spacing. (See *Specific Skills Guide* — Running.) |
| | 2 Soft running, change direction on signal and run and jump and land. | 2 Awareness of moving into space and springing up from landing. |
| **Body preparation** | 1 Sitting, legs in front, and stroke the inside of one leg with the sole of the foot of the other leg. | 1 Hip mobility. |
| | 2 Stand up: raise heels and lower them, alternately. | 2 Ankle mobility. |
| **Floor activities** | 1 *On the spot* try out all different ways of jumping. | 1 Remind of bending into immediate stretching of legs. |
| | 2 All bounce: 2 feet to 2 feet: balanced landing and spring up. Repeat several times. | 2 Importance of balanced landing and resilient rebound. |
| | 3 Repeat 2 with high bounce preceding landing. | 3 Explosive stretching of ankles and legs, held until touchdown for landing. |
| | 4 Examine other ways of using feet in jumping.<br>2 → 1 (two feet to one foot):<br>1 → 2: 1 → 1: 1 → same. | 4 Problem of landing on 1 leg — turn landing foot out and get other foot down quickly. |

| Content | Teaching points |
|---|---|
| 5 Select 3 of the 5 basic jumps and link together. | 5 Practise for accurate repetition. Then remind of stretching and landings. (Refer *Specific Skills Guide* — Jumping). |

**Final activity** In pairs, X lies on floor making body VERY tense (like a board). Y squats and tries to turn X over. Change role.

Show this with a child first and emphasize care. Place hands at chest (A) and hips (B). Requires much tension throughout body.

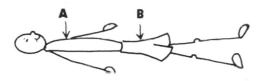

Then:
Stand well.

# YEAR 3

**Autumn Term:** **TRAVELLING**
**Session 5:** **With jumping**

| | Content | Teaching points |
|---|---|---|
| **Warm up** | 1 Soft running, on command jump, land and continue running. | 1 Precise placement of feet — good body carriage. |
| | 2 Repeat, changing direction after each springing action. | 2 Finish off the spring, land and spring up again before changing direction with the next run. |
| **Body preparation** | 1 Kneeling, sit on heels, alternate arm circling backwards. | 1 Sitting back restricts action to the shoulder joint. |
| | 2 Lie on back, raise and lower legs alternately. | 2 Helps strengthen hip flexors and stomach. |
| **Apparatus activities** | Benches and mats as in Sessions 2 and 3. | |
| | 1 Stand on bench, jump off to land on mat — land spring up again. | 1 Use of arms throughout. Good landing. |
| | 2 Approach bench, take off from floor and land on bench on two feet, spring off. | 2 Beginning of feeling of hurdle step — floor (1 foot) bench (2 feet). (See *Specific Skills Guide* — Hurdle Step) |
| | 3 Jumping on to and off bench. Show 3 different jumps. | 3 Preparation for jump requires bending of legs, then explosive stretch and lift. |

| Content | Teaching points |
|---|---|
| 4 Using your bench and mat make a pattern of jumping and running which changes direction. Try to make it smooth and flowing. | 4 Patterns need to be quite short in order to concentrate on fluency. Select good examples to explain this point. |

**Final activity**  Lie on back, feet under bench (knees bent). Curl up to place forehead on knees 10 times.

Strengthens stomach.

Apparatus away.
Stand well.

# YEAR 3

**TRAVELLING**
**On hands and feet**

|  | Content | Teaching points |
|---|---|---|
| **Warm up** | 1 Emphasis on one aspect of running. | 1 (See *Specific Skills Guide —* Running.) |
|  | 2 Soft running, on signal change to side slipping. | 2 Feel differences in leg action when sideways movement happening. |
| **Body preparation** | 1 Practise bunny jumps (movements from feet to hands to feet). | 1 Controlled and precise. Spread fingers, flatten hands, lock elbows. Keep head forward initially to prevent toppling over. (Use good example from class to make this point.) |
|  | 2 Kneel, hands on floor. Reach under one arm with the other twisting to reach as far as possible. Repeat using other arm. | 2 Trunk mobility. |
| **Floor activities** | 1 Experiment with different ways of travelling on hands and feet. | 1 Articulate on combination, directions, tummy up/down, etc. |
|  | 2 Repeat, trying to stretch more. Be clear and controlled. | 2 Transfer weight with control as hand(s)/foot (feet) touch-down. |
|  | 3 Practise cat springs (*i.e.*: 2 feet to 2 hands to 2 feet). | 3 Clear directional placement of hands. Push from feet. |
|  | 4 As 3 placing feet ahead of hands by twisting hips to the side. | 4 Raise hips high, twist and prepare feet for landing. |

| Content | Teaching points |
|---|---|
| 5 Using 2 hands and 2 feet travel by turning stomach up, stomach down. | 5 High lift of initiating arm or leg, reach as far as possible. Tension to maintain control. |
| 6 Practise a different form of travelling on hands and feet. | 6 Does it require thrust? Or careful placement? |
| 7 Travel continuously, using hands and feet combinations, keep changing method of travel. | 7 Emphasize stretching and thrust. |

**Final activity**

As a class, squat jump 3 forwards, 3 to the right, 3 to the left and 3 backwards.

Keep backs straight. Do it rhythmically and it will help. Good leg strengthener. Emphasize control.

Then:
Stand well.

# YEAR 3

**Autumn Term:** **TRAVELLING**
**Session 7:** **On hands and feet**

| | Content | Teaching points |
|---|---|---|
| **Warm up** | 1 Soft running, on signal change to side slipping. | 1 Feel differences in leg action when sideways movement happening. |
| | 2 Soft running. On 'One' change to side slipping, on 'Two' fast moving on hands and feet together, on 'Three' two star jumps. | 2 Crisp, precise changes between actions. |
| **Body preparation** | 1 Lie on back, flatten back, raise legs, part and close legs. Repeat × 5. | 1 Stomach and hip strengthener. Back must be flat. |
| | 2 a) toe bending, stretching and separating<br>b) sit cross-legged, put head on floor between knees. | 2 Ensure full mobility. |
| **Floor activities** | 1 Travel continuously, using hands and feet combinations, keep changing method of travel. | 1 Emphasize stretching and thrust. (Remind of last session's work). |
| | 2 If necessary, identify the differences explored last session. | |

|  | **Content** | **Teaching points** |
|---|---|---|

**Apparatus activities**

In 7 groups
1 and 2: stool or stacking table,
inclined plank and mat
3: Bar box, inclined bench and
mat
4 and 5: climbing frame: 2
inclined planks and 2 mats
6 and 7: benches: mats either side

frame
against wall

1 Find different starting places.
  How can you travel using
  hands and feet on your
  apparatus?

1 Remind children of ideas
  practised on floor.

2 Begin on apparatus, grip it
  with hands and push to land on
  floor on feet.

2 Ensure landing area is clear.
  Hold firmly. Prepare feet for
  landing.

3 Cross any part of apparatus.
  Use hands only on apparatus.

3 Use floor work ideas here.
  How high up apparatus can
  this be done? Stretching and
  thrust needed.

**Final activity**

Apparatus away.
Stand well.

**Apparatus pattern**

Group 4

Group 5

Group 3

Group 1

Group 2

Group 6

Group 7

27

# YEAR 3

**Autumn Term:** **TRAVELLING**
**Sessions 8 and 9:** **On hands and feet**

| | Content | Teaching points |
|---|---|---|
| **Warm up** | 1 Soft running on 'One' change to side slipping, on 'Two' fast moving on hands and feet together, on 'Three' two star jumps. | 1 Crisp, clear changes. |
| | 2 Without travelling too far practise moving from feet to hands to feet. | 2 Ensure correct hand placement. Try to feel you are really taking your weight on your arms. Heads looking forward. |
| **Body preparation** | 1 Kneel, hands on floor, and alternately arch and round back (happy cat/angry cat). | 1 These both develop trunk mobility. |
| | 2 Ditto, raise knee to meet forehead and then foot to touch back of head. | 2 Slowly. |
| **Apparatus activities** | Apparatus as for Session 7. | |
| | *Groups 1 and 2* Travel up plank: hands gripping plank: feet crossing floor → plank → floor → plank. Gentle spring from stool or table to mat, and then land. | Preparation of feet for each touch down. Work hard in arms to assist legs. |

| **Content** | **Teaching points** |
|---|---|

*Group 3*
Travel as far up bench as possible with hands gripping bench, pushing feet from one side to the other (not touching bench). Continue any way to top, controlled jump to mat.

See Teaching Points for Groups 1 and 2.

*Groups 4 and 5*
Remaining wholly on plank travel up it feet → hands → feet. Poise on frame and jump down to land on mat.

Reach far ahead and bring feet carefully close to hands. High end of bench no more than 1m high. Look to see floor space clear before jumping from frame.

*Groups 6 and 7*
Travel along bench, gripping it with hands, swinging the legs over from side to side (one leg after the other).

Begin gently, gradually getting hips higher. Lunge step forward to place hands on bench.

*Note*: These are all quite specific tasks and as such will begin to demand quality from the children. (Give out tasks in turn, quite clearly to whole class *or use task cards*.)

**Final activity**

Apparatus away.
Stand well.

*Task Card Example*:

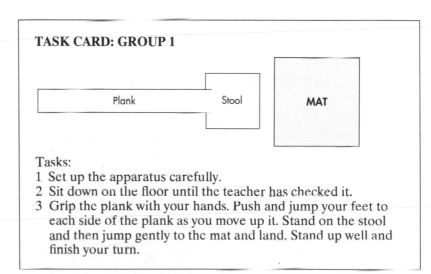

**TASK CARD: GROUP 1**

Plank — Stool — MAT

Tasks:
1 Set up the apparatus carefully.
2 Sit down on the floor until the teacher has checked it.
3 Grip the plank with your hands. Push and jump your feet to each side of the plank as you move up it. Stand on the stool and then jump gently to the mat and land. Stand up well and finish your turn.

# YEAR 3

**Autumn Term:** **TRAVELLING**
**Session 10:** **Linking actions**

| | Content | Teaching points |
|---|---|---|
| **Warm up** | 1 Travelling on feet changing activity on command. Running, skipping, bouncing. Repeat on the spot. | 1 Good body carriage. Precise feet and ankles. |
| | 2 Change freely from moving on the spot to travelling. | 2 *Note*: it is important that children make decisions when to change the activity freely. Encourage 'bounce' and 'lift'. |
| **Body preparation** | 1 Stand about 1 metre from wall and push away — Repeat × 5. | 1 Push strength. |
| | 2 a) Ankle bending and stretching <br> b) Feet astride — hip circling <br> c) Kneeling, walk hands as far round as possible to alternate sides. | 2 Ensure full mobility. |
| **Floor activities** | 1 Revise running, jumping and landing. | See Sessions 1–4. |
| | 2 Practise an *action phrase* of run, jump, land and jump. | Remind of 5 basic jumps. (Practise again if necessary). |
| | 3 Repeat, smoothly moving from one part of the phrase to the next. | Think about next action *before* it begins. |
| | 4 Try out ways of first travelling across floor on hands and feet before going into the jump/ land/jump part of the phrase. | Remind of actions learnt in Session 6. Can they move smoothly into the jumps? Try several ideas. |

| Content | Teaching points |
|---|---|
| | |

**Content**

5 Repeat and practise whole phrase.
(*i.e.* hands/feet action — jump — land — jump).

**Teaching points**

Repetition *essential* for quality. Need stretching, tension and thrust as appropriate. Clear beginning to phrase and clear, still ending.

**Final activity**

All class lies on stomach. Keeping feet fixed see who is first to stand up.

Then:
Stand well.

Arm strengthening exercise.

# YEAR 3

## Autumn Term: Assessment and consolidation sessions

The children should now have experienced:

1  General ways of travelling on feet; running, skipping, jumping, etc.

2  Different kinds of jumps (2 feet to 2 feet etc.)

3  Some aspects of travelling on hands and feet in different combinations. (Catsprings etc.)

They should be able to apply these 3 aspects to work on floor, on benches and mats and on other simple pieces of apparatus.

They should be beginning to link together movements from these 3 aspects on floor and on apparatus, and develop ACTION PHRASES.

The next sessions therefore should make good any noted weaknesses in these aspects of TRAVELLING returning to any of the Autumn Term Sessions 1–10.

Any aspects particularly enjoyed by the children may be repeated.

**For your notes and comments:**

# YEAR 3

**Spring Term:** **BALANCE**
**Session 1:** **What is balance?**

| | Content | Teaching points |
|---|---|---|
| **Warm up** | 1 Free running, changing direction at will. | 1 Relaxed style — awareness of space — good carriage. |
| | 2 Run a few steps jump and land — hold the balance. Repeat several times. | 2 Point out that it is easier to hold the balance if landing is made with feet slightly apart. (Wider base of support). Question children as to why they may be losing balance. It may be because:<br>(a) The base of support is not wide enough.<br>(b) There is too much forward momentum which takes the centre of gravity outside the base of support. |
| **Body preparation** | 1 Sitting legs straight in front. Gently press trunk down to legs (press, press, press and relax). | 1 Easy pressure. |
| | 2 Hop on alternate legs 10 times each. | 2 Helps jump strength. |

|  | **Content** | **Teaching points** |
|---|---|---|
| **Floor activities** | 1 In your own space try to find different body parts on which you can hold your weight and be still. | 1 Articulate the different answers the children are showing. |
| | 2 Select different responses from different children and all try these. | 2 Expect large body parts — seat, tummy/Combinations of small parts — feet and 1 hand/Parts on same side of body/Parts on opposite side of body, etc. |
| | 3 Children sit on the floor in a space. Ask children which parts of their body are touching the floor. (Probably their bottom and 2 feet.) | 3 Be quite still and hold your body straight. |
| | 4 Now ask children to take their feet and hands off floor and sit on bottom only. | 4 Ask why it was easier to balance with bottom and feet touching the floor than it is with feet off the floor. |
| | 5 Children now try to balance on their bottoms slowly extending their legs to get into a V sit position. | 5 Feel what the body has to do to keep the balance. Try to get a 'perched' feel. |
| | 6 Children now balance on other large parts of the body. | 6 Try to get as much of the body off the floor as is appropriate. Keep the body tension. |
| | 7 Link balances on various large parts without using hands. Start with moving from 'bottom' to 'side' to 'stomach'. Clearly show balance on each part. | 7 Emphasize slow controlled movement between balances. Extend body away from point of balance. The children should be able to perform and repeat a simple sequence of balances with control and good tension. |
| **Final activity** | Front support position with feet still, walk the hands round the compass. | Arm strength is developed. |
| | Then:<br>Stand well. | |

# YEAR 3

**Spring Term:**    **BALANCE**
**Session 2:**    **What is balance?**

|  | Content | Teaching points |
|---|---|---|
| **Warm up** | 1 Soft running. On 'Up' do a tucked jump, on 'Wide' a star jump and on 'Long' a stretch jump. | 1 Ensure jump is clearly executed before running continues.<br>Clarity of body shape. |
| **Body preparation** | 1 Sit, stretch legs as wide as is comfortable, rock onto back and press legs gently wider. | 1 Hands press inside of thighs. Keep legs straight. |
| | 2 a) Ankle bending and stretching<br>b) Toe bending, stretching and separating. | 2 Concentrate on good mobility. |
| **Floor activities** | 1 Revise the pattern of linked balances from last session. | 1 Large parts, changing without putting hands on floor. |
| | 2 Find balances on small body parts. | 2 Look for different numbers of parts touching floor. What happens to the rest of the body? Stretch it away from the base and hold a clear position before you try another one. |
| | 3 Link a balance on a small part(s) with one on a large part. | 3 Try to feel that sense of 'perching' before you change balance. Keep the tension. |
| | 4 Repeat but with different balances. | 4 As above. |

| Content | Teaching points |
|---|---|

*Mat Work*    Children in groups using all the mats.

| | |
|---|---|
| 1  Begin about 3 metres from the mat. Travel to the mat and finish on edge in a clear balance. Cross the mat and balance again. Travel away from mat. | 1  Remind children (sit and discuss) of work on TRAVELLING already covered. Try to encourage<br>a)  variety<br>b)  'perched', stretched balance positions.<br>*Note*:  Take each part of this long task in stages and work on each separately and then put it back together again as a phrase. |

**Final activity**    In same groups as above squat jumping around the mat and back again.

Leg strengthening.

Mats away.
Stand well.

# YEAR 3

**Spring Term:** **BALANCE**
**Session 3:** **Related to shape**

| | Content | Teaching points |
|---|---|---|
| **Warm up** | 1 Run, jump, land and balance. Repeat several times. | 1 Do not allow landing to detract from a good jumping action. Clarity essential. |
| **Body preparation** | 1 Kneel and *sit back on heels*. Slowly rotate arms backwards (brushing ears) trying to reach far behind. | 1 Sitting back restricts activity to the shoulder joint. |
| | 2 Sit, legs straight. Rotate ankles reaching as far as possible in each direction. | 2 Ensure that the children get full ankle mobility. |
| **Floor activities** | 1 Balance on large parts of the body showing first a narrow stretched shape and then (on same parts) a wide stretched shape. | 1 Does it feel different? Did you have to do anything else to hold the balance? |
| | 2 Repeat with less of the body on the floor (*e.g.* 1 hip). | 2 Again what differences do you notice? |
| | 3 Begin balanced in a tucked shape, slowly stretch out from this position, then change to a different tucked balance. | 3 Still try to feel 'perched' in each balance. Use arms and legs to help you get into the last balance. |
| | 4 Develop a pattern of 3 balances showing tucked, narrow, stretched and wide shapes. Try to move clearly between each balance. | 4 Remind children of different bases. Discuss the different ways children move between the balances. |

| Content | Teaching points |
|---|---|
| **Content** | **Teaching points** |
| 5  Can you change the order and still make the pattern smooth? | 5  Children will need to sort out different ways of moving between the balances. |

**Final activity**

| | |
|---|---|
| Pairs 'Duck Fighting'. | Pairs: crouch position facing each other. Children place hands in front of their chests and try to unbalance each other using flats of hands. They must stay in crouch position. (Leg strength). |
| Then:<br>Stand well. | |

# YEAR 3

**Spring Term:** **BALANCE**
**Session 4:** **Related to apparatus**

| | Content | Teaching points |
|---|---|---|
| **Warm up** | 1 Running, changing on command to side slipping. Repeat. | 1 Relaxed bouncy run, followed by strong sideways 'Drive' in second activity. |
| **Body preparation** | 1 On all fours, alternately arch back and round back (happy cat/angry cat). | 1 Back mobility. |
| | 2 Straddle sitting, press tummy down to floor. | 2 Easy pressure. |
| **Apparatus activities** | Benches and box tops and low nesting tables, with mats. Space out evenly with mats well away from benches, etc. | |
| | 1 Practise balancing in different ways using your apparatus. | 1 An exploratory task — articulate to the class the different responses. |
| | 2 (Two tasks). Some of you try out different balances on the mat. Others try balances on benches etc. Change role. | 2 Get children to try all the ideas learnt *i.e.* sessions 1–3 *i.e.* different body parts — different shapes. Go through these, in turn if necessary. (Warn children to be aware of others.) |
| | 3 Try now to find balances where you are partly on the floor (or mat) and partly on, or against the apparatus. | 3 (Be aware of children simply resting on apparatus.) |

| Content | Teaching points |
|---|---|
| 4 Jump onto bench and balance. Find a way of changing to a new balance as in 3, then move from this to a new balance on mat or floor. | 4 A structured sequence trying to emphasize the different *ways* of using apparatus with balancing and also trying to highlight links between balances. |

---

**Final activity**

| | |
|---|---|
| Using benches or wall frame. Bend and straighten arms 10 times. | Stronger children will be able to do this arm strengthening exercise on benches. Those less strong *higher* up wall frame.

Keep body tense. |

Apparatus away.
Stand well.

*Note*: There are 4 simple possibilities to encourage when linking BALANCE with apparatus.
1 Balancing *wholly on* a piece of apparatus.
2 Balancing, touching more than one piece of apparatus.
3 Balancing, touching floor and apparatus. (especially getting the children to GRIP the apparatus where appropriate to develop more ideas).
4 Balancing away from the apparatus.

# YEAR 3

**Spring Term:** **TRAVELLING**
**Session 5:** **On large parts — emphasizing sliding**

| | Content | Teaching points |
|---|---|---|
| **Warm up** | 1 3 runs on spot followed by 3 bounding leaps. Repeat several times. | 1 Feel the difference when the back leg drives for the bounding leap. |
| **Body preparation** | 1 Bouncing on the spot increasing height. | 1 Feel full stretch. Repeat as appropriate to help develop strength. |
| | 2 a) Standing, stretch alternate arms upwards<br>b) Standing, kick hand held at shoulder height in various directions. | 2 Shoulder and hip mobility respectively. |
| **Floor activities** | 1 Choose a starting position close to the floor (*e.g.* knees, seat, shoulders, etc.). Travel across the floor using rolling, sliding or rocking movements. | 1 Articulate the various responses of the children to the class. |
| | 2 Repeat, ensuring that all three different actions are included. | 2 Stop and discuss the differences between the 3 actions. |
| | 3 Repeat and on command change from sliding to rolling to rocking. | 3 Essential to hold the body *clearly* and *firmly* in correct position during the whole action. |
| | 4 *Sliding:* find different parts of the body you can slide on. Is it possible to slide on these using PUSHING movements and PULLING movements? | 4 Parts not touching the floor must be extended and held with control during the action. |

| Content | Teaching points |
|---|---|
| 5 Stretch out on your side, use your arms. a) to push you into sliding then b) pull you into sliding. | 5 As above — really stretch legs off the floor. |
| 6 Try this on scat with legs high in the air. Try on tummy with the rest of the body fully stretched. | 6 Tight muscle control in stomach and legs. |
| 7 Find another part or parts you can slide on. | 7 As above. |
| 8 Make up a pattern to include 2 balances, 1 sliding action, a run and a jump. | 8 An essential 'stage' in trying to bring different aspects already taught to bear on this session's emphasis. *Note*: you have *not* determined the order of actions. |

**Final activity**

| | |
|---|---|
| 1 Prone lying — get up keeping feet in one spot. | 1 Arm strengthener. |

Then:
Stand well.

# YEAR 3

**Spring Term:** TRAVELLING
**Session 6:** On large body parts emphasizing general rolling and rocking

|  | Content | Teaching points |
|---|---|---|
| **Warm up** | 1 Free running. | 1 (Check with *Specific Skills Guide* — Running, if necessary.) |
|  | 2 Travel feet to hands to feet. | 2 Thrust strongly from legs, have arms ready to receive weight. |
| **Body preparation** | 1 All fours. Lift one leg and try to touch back of head with toes, then tuck leg under and try to touch knee onto forehead. Change leg. Repeat 5 times. | 1 Back mobility. Ensure slow stretching. |
|  | 2 Lie on back, raise legs and chest to V sit. Repeat 5 times. | 2 Increase number if appropriate. |
| **Mat work** | 1 Begin on shoulders, roll down your back and finish still on your seat — then roll back again to shoulders. | 1 To make children aware that rolling is the continuous action along adjacent body parts. Long curve of spine. Rest of body *held clearly*. It begins to look like a rocking action. |
|  | 2 Roll across mats on hips only, turning over once. | 2 Legs must be active in keeping action moving. Tension throughout body essential. |
|  | 3 Roll sideways tucked up tightly then stretch out and roll back again. | 3 Feel difference between the 2 body shapes. |

| Content | Teaching points |
|---|---|
| 4 Roll sideways finishing on your seat then roll up onto shoulders. | 4 Constant awareness of the use of legs. |
| 5 Rocking is only used to build up speed or power for another movement, but first practise rocking on different body parts and in different directions. | 5 Try to draw out forward/back/side/side, and diagonal actions. On front, back, hips, shoulders, etc. |
| 6 Rock across seat from side to side to then take you quickly into a roll. | 6 Call out 'rock and rock and rock and ROLL!' Let voice suggest build up to begin with. Build up is *vital*. |
| 7 Find a different rocking action to take you into a rolling action. | 7 As above if necessary. Clear held body shape. |

**Final activity**

In turn squat jump onto and off mat: centre → back → centre → left centre → right centre → forward.

Try to only use 1 bounce per direction change.

Mats away.
Stand well.

*Note*: General rolling actions will have been explored in the 4–7 age phase. The difference here is the need for absolute clarity of the body shape which is a pre-requisite for many related actions. Additionally, the children should be *knowing* the differences in their movements.

# YEAR 3

**Spring Term:**   **TRAVELLING**
**Session 7:**   **Introducing forward roll**

This session is somewhat different in that it relates directly to skill teaching

| | Content | Teaching points |
|---|---|---|
| **Warm up** | 1 Free running with change of direction. | 1 Emphasize footwork as direction changes. |
| | 2 On each direction change, change the action. | 2 Expect hops, jumps, skips, side slipping, etc. |
| **Body preparation** | 1 On all fours, alternately arch back and hunch back (happy cat/angry cat). | 1 Back mobility. |
| | 2 Lie on stomach, hold hands behind back and raise chest. Repeat 5 times. | 2 To develop back strength. Press toes down. |
| **Apparatus activities** | Use all mats: children in equal groups. It will be necessary for children to take turns. | |
| | 1 Rock backwards and forwards. | 1 Heels close to bottom and chin to chest. (See *Specific Skills Guide* — Forward Roll.) |
| | 2 Repeat 1, but now come to standing as feet touch down. | 2 Arms reach forward. It may be helpful to reach for a partner's hands to encourage this action. |

| Content | Teaching points |
|---|---|
| 3 Stand feet astride, hands on floor in front of feet, shoulder width apart. Tuck chin to chest, lower top of shoulders to the floor and tip over to roll. | 3 Children should take their weight on their hands and transfer carefully on to shoulders. Try to encourage stretched legs during roll, tucking as standing phase begins. This should be a controlled action. (See Fig. 4, (c) *Specific Skills Guide* — Forward Roll.) |
| 4 Those who master 3 begin roll from squat position. Those who are not ready continue with 3. | 4 Initial movement therefore goes *forward*. For some children the problem may be solved by trying the 'helping' activities described in the *Specific Skills Guide*. |
| 5 Free practice, aiming for precision and control. | 5 Don't let the children rush at this stage. |

*Note*: Some children may get dizzy. If this happens introduce an alternative activity (*e.g.* springing and landing from benches).

## Final activity

Mats away.
Stand well.

*Note*: See *Introduction* to Section 2: *Skill* on page 7.

# YEAR 3

**Spring Term:** TRAVELLING
**Session 8:** Rocking, rolling and sliding — related to apparatus

| | Content | Teaching points |
|---|---|---|
| **Warm up** | 1 Run gently around hall, zig-zagging as you go. | 1 Careful changes of direction, controlled actions. |
| | 2 Repeat but more rapidly. | 2 Positive footwork and good spacing. |
| **Body preparation** | 1 Standing broad jumps × 5. | 1 Strengthens legs. |
| | 2 a) heel raising and lowering alternately<br>b) kneeling, hands on ground, circling alternate legs. | 2 Ensure good mobility. |
| **Apparatus activities** | Arrange as in session 7 Autumn Term (Page 27) | |

*General tasks for all apparatus*

| | Content | Teaching points |
|---|---|---|
| | 1 Find places on the apparatus where you can travel using rocking, rolling and sliding. | 1 Remind about rocking being used to build up (to get on or off maybe). |
| | 2 Begin on the apparatus, slide to touch floor and then roll away. Use forward roll if appropriate. | 2 Emphasize roll to really *travel away*. |
| | 3 Travel onto, through or along, and off apparatus using a sliding action, then a rocking action to take you into a roll. | 3 Try to develop continually here → slide → rock → roll and encourage *travelling* not movement on the spot. |

| Content | Teaching points |
|---|---|
| 4 Practise rolling along (up and down) benches using hips only, travelling sideways. | 4 Lively use of rest of body to keep balanced and controlled. Legs will help if kept fairly wide apart. |
| 5 Slide down or along the bench on different body parts, keeping rest of body *above* the bench. | 5 Encourage variety — vitally important to maintain good body tension — no collapse. |

## Final activity

Apparatus away.
Stand well.

*Note*: Task Cards could be used here.

# YEAR 3

**Spring Term:** **TRAVELLING**
**Sessions 9 and 10:** **Rocking, rolling and sliding — related to apparatus**

|  | Content | Teaching points |
|---|---|---|
| **Warm up** | 1 Running, changing on command to side slipping. | 1 Relaxed bouncy run followed by strong sideways 'drive' in second activity. |
| **Body preparation** | 1 Happy cat/angry cat.<br>2 Straddle sitting, pressing tummy to ground. | 1 Back mobility.<br>2 Gentle pressure only — not forced. |

**Apparatus activities**

*Reminder: As Session 8.*
Groups 1 and 2: Stools or stacking tables, inclined planks to floor, mats.
Group 3: Bar box, inclined plank, mat.
Group 4: Climbing frame, 2 inclined planks, about 12" high from ground, side by side, one mat on top, one on floor.
Group 5 and 6: Benches, mats on either side.

The tasks are specific to different apparatus arrangements — give *one* task for each section first, then the second. When children can change at will from the first to the second, they are ready to move to a different section.

*Or* use TASK CARDS.

Give the children enough time to master the tasks. Use the 2 full lessons for this aspect of the work (or more if needed).

*Groups 1 and 2*

| 1 Travel to mat: roll across mat, spring up onto stool or task. Slide down plank. | 1 Explosive spring. Tension in body during slide. |
|---|---|
| 2 Make up a different sequence using this apparatus. | 2 Relate it to all the different travelling actions already explored. |

| Content | Teaching points |
|---|---|
| *Group 3*<br>1 Practise rolls (or part rolls as on mats) on box top. | 1 Grip box as appropriate. Keep control in *legs* to avoid over rotating. |
| 2 Make up a sequence involving a jump, roll and sliding action using your apparatus. | |
| *Group 4*<br>Teach backward roll. | (See *Specific Skills Guide* — Backward Roll.)<br>Teacher should control this station and ensure all the groups move through in 2 sessions. (Station = one apparatus grouping). |
| *Groups 5 and 6*<br>1 Slide along bench (a little way) on shoulders — legs high. Grip bench, twist to touch down feet on floor and roll across mat. | 1 Hold onto bench firmly until feet touch mat. |
| 2 Jump on to bench, jump off, land roll into a balance. | 2 Land in control before moving into the roll. |

**Final activity**

| | |
|---|---|
| Children lean (with tension) against a piece of apparatus, arms straight. Bend and straighten arms 6 times. Keeping feet in same place. | Arm strengthener. Stronger children can do this fairly low down. |
| Apparatus away.<br>Stand well. | |

# YEAR 3

**Assessment and consolidation sessions**

The children should now have experienced:
1 Basic principles of balance in relation to taking weight on large and small body parts.
2 Variety of balances held with changed body shape.
3 Movement between balances.
4 Balance on, against and off the apparatus.
5 Travelling generally on large body parts (rocking, sliding and rolling).
6 Specific lessions on rolling (Forward roll and backward roll).
7 Ways of using 5 and 6 on large apparatus.

The next sessions should therefore, as before, make good any noted weaknesses in these aspects of BALANCE and TRAVELLING by returning to any of the Spring Term Sessions 1–10.

Do also repeat aspects the children have particularly enjoyed.

**For your notes and comments:**

# YEAR 4

**Autumn Term:** **TRAVELLING**
**Session 1:** **Jumping and rolling**

This session (and Sessions 2 and 3) direct the children's attention quite specifically towards practising the basic skills of jumping and rolling. The intention is that through the directed skill-orientated tasks the children will have the opportunity to revise these aspects which were introduced in Year 3.

| | Content | Teaching points |
|---|---|---|
| **Warm up** | 1 Free running with change of direction. | 1 Precise and clear changes. |
| | 2 Short run, jump, land and spring up again. | 2 Stretch in air and complete landing fully before running on. |
| **Body preparation** | 1 Bounce on spot, gradually increasing the height. | 1 Repeat as appropriate to develop strength. |
| | 2 Caterpillar walk. | 2 Fix hands and gradually bring straight legs closer to the hands. Then walk hands away from feet. |
| **Floor activities** | 1 Jumping on the spot with a $\frac{1}{4}$ turn. | 1 (*See Specific Skills Guide —* Jumping.) There should be an emphasis on a correct arm action and a movement of the head and shoulders in the direction of the turn. The children can 'jump round the compass points.' |
| | 2 *Short* run, jump, land and spring up again. | 2 Landing to emphasize coming straight back up. |
| | 3 Repeat 2 adding $\frac{1}{4}$ turn to jump. | 3 *Short* run — think ahead. Spring *up* straight from landing. |

56

|  | Content | Teaching points |
|---|---|---|
| **Mat work** | Use all the mats — children in groups | |
| | General tasks for all groups: | |
| | 1 Revise forward roll. | 1 (See *Specific Skills Guide* — Rolling.) |
| | 2 Teach next stage of backward roll. | 2 (Relate to Sessions 9 and 10, Spring Term Year 3). (See *Specific Skills Guide* — Backward Roll.) |
| | 3 Practise other ways of rolling. | 3 Expect rolling across hips, barrel rolls, etc. Emphasize correct shape. |
| | 4 On your mat make up a pattern of 3 rolls which cross the mat, continuously changing direction. Let the final roll bring you to your feet and finish with a jump (neat landing). | 4 Preparation for next roll at end of previous roll. |
| | Mats away | |
| **Final activity** | 1 In 2s — trying to turn partner over. | 1 Feel tension throughout the body. |
| | Then: Stand well. | |

# YEAR 4

**Autumn Term:**   **TRAVELLING**
**Sessions 2 and 3:**   **Jumping and rolling**

| | Content | Teaching points |
|---|---|---|
| **Warm up** | 1 Running alternating with hopping and skipping. | 1 Change the action clearly and with control. |
| | 2 Run, jump and land, springing straight up again. | 2 Short run, jumps should be fully completed before running on. |
| **Body preparation** | 1 Lie on front, raise chest and legs at the same time. Repeat × 5. | 1 Hold lifted position for a count of 3. |
| | 2 Straddle sit, press tummy to floor. | 2 Easy pressure. |
| | 3 Kneel, sitting back on heels alternately circle arms backwards. | 3 Ensure full mobility. |
| **Apparatus activities** | Give the children sufficient time to practise each task to their and your satisfaction. | |
| | Group 1: Begin on bench. Jump with $\frac{1}{4}$ turn from bench to land on mat. | 1 Again emphasize correct arm action and correct movement of head and shoulders and controlled landing. |
| | Group 2: Travel up plank gripping plank with hands, feet changing from one side to the other. | 2 Strong push from legs and work hard on arms. |
| | Group 3: Short approach run to bench, take off 1 foot to land on two feet on bench, jump to land on mat. Vary the shape of the jump in the air. | 3 Try to encourage 'hurdle' step approach. Again tension in body to hold clear shape. (Chalk circle on floor may help). (See *Specific Skills Guide* — Jumping.) |

| Content | Teaching points |
|---|---|
| Group 4: Practise forward and backward rolls, trying to vary the shape of the legs during the roll. | 4 Combination of legs together/apart/bent/straight. *Note*: Hand placement for straddle roll. (See *Specific Skills Guide* — Rolling.) |
| Group 5: Squat jump on to box. Spring off showing clear stretched body shape in air before good landing. | 5 Strong push from legs essential for squat jump. Children can squat up on knees if they have difficulty getting their feet through on to the box. |
| Group 6: Practise straddle forward roll carefully down the slope. | 6 Feet are placed at either side of the benches when finishing the roll. (See *Specific Skills Guide* — Rolling.) |

Children should be discouraged from hurrying through these activities. The aim is for quality/skill and so control and concentration is essential.

TASK CARDS may be useful here. (See Year 3, sessions 8 and 9.)

| | | |
|---|---|---|
| **Final activity** | In same groups, follow my leader squat jumping around the mat. | Mats may need to be pulled away from benches etc. |

Apparatus away.
Stand well.

## Apparatus pattern

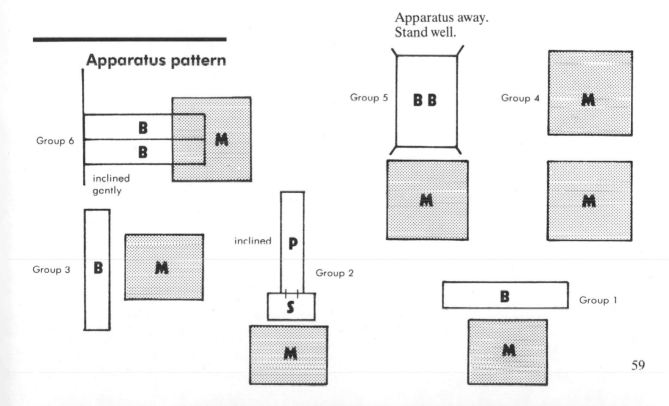

# YEAR 4

**Autumn Term:** **BALANCE**
**Session 4:** **With travelling into and out of balance**

| | Content | Teaching points |
|---|---|---|
| **Warm up** | 1 Free running. | 1 Emphasize one aspect of running (See *Specific Skills Guide* — Running.) |
| | 2 3 bounces followed by $\frac{1}{4}$ turn jump. Repeat 4 times. | 2 Ensure correct use of arms during turn. |
| **Body preparation** | 1 Straddle sit, rock to back and gently press thighs apart a little wider. | 1 Place hands inside thighs and ensure easy pressure. |
| | 2 Front support (press up position), walk arms round the feet. | 2 Keep the feet fixed. |
| **Floor activities** | 1 Revise the different parts of the body on which you can balance. | 1 Small parts, large parts, combinations etc. |
| | 2 Repeat, stretching further and holding clear body shapes. | 2 Revise the feeling of what is balance. |
| | 3 All hold a shoulder balance. Use a roll to bring you out of balance and on to your feet. | 3 Point out the different directions the roll can take. Body must prepare itself for the roll → feet. Repeat several times. |
| | 4 Find another balance and practise ways of rolling out of this balance. | 4 Show one or two to encourage variety. |

| Content | Teaching points |
|---|---|
| 5 Find other ways of getting out of balance. | 5 Discuss other ways of travelling apart from rolling, (jumping, wheeling, by using hands/feet, rocking, sliding, etc.) |
| 6 Show travel — balance — travel — balance. | 6 Clear method of travelling into the first balance, use the next method of travelling to take you smoothly out of the 1st balance, and across the floor into the 2nd balance. |
| 7 Take each part of 6 in turn and practise. Then put whole together again. | 7 Again a 'clarifying' strategy to help children focus on their work. |

**Final activity**

Lie face down. Raise head and chest, clap 5 times and lower head and chest. Repeat.

Back strengthener.

Then:
Stand well.

# YEAR 4

**Autumn Term:**
**Sessions 5 and 6:**

## BALANCE
## Introducing headstand

These lessons introduce specific teaching of the headstand (as it relates to the unit BALANCE), in the form of a class activity. Group work revises activities already taught.

| | Content | Teaching points |
|---|---|---|
| **Warm up** | 1 Run spring land and spring up again. Repeat several times. Add $\frac{1}{4}$ turn as appropriate. | 1 Short run for efficient take off. Clear stretched body shape in air. |
| **Body preparation** | 1 Travel feet/hands/feet trying to take weight *fully* on hands. | 1 Keep head forward, push strongly from hands. Aim is to *work* on arms. |
| | 2 All fours, touch knees to forehead then foot to back of head — 3 times. Repeat with other foot. | 2 An exercise for back mobility. Encourage children to stretch hard. |
| | 3 Caterpillar walk. | 3 Fix hands and gradually walk feet to hands, then hands away. |

## Apparatus activities

Mats — children in groups

| | | |
|---|---|---|
| | 1 Teach headstand. | 1 (See *Specific Skills Guide* — Headstand.) |

SPECIFIC TASKS    6 groups (Plan as for Sessions 2 and 3)

*Group Work*

| | |
|---|---|
| Group 1: Practise first crossing bench taking weight on hands ... then practice the *hurdle step* onto and off the bench. | 1 Check grip on bench for first task, fingers pointing *up the length* of the bench. For hurdle stop (see *Specific Skills Guide* — Jumping.) |
| Group 2: Gently run up plank and jump from stool to land on mat. | 2 Purposeful run. NB. check landing area is (a) SAFE (b) CLEAR |

| Content | Teaching points |
|---|---|
| Group 3: Jump from bench and take landing into a roll. | 3 Landing should first be controlled before going into roll. Bring roll back to feet. |
| Group 4: Practise forward and backward rolls (varying shape of legs where possible). | 4 Trying now for fluency and good quality. |
| Group 5: Squat jump on to box, jump off and land on mat. Vary body shape in the air. | 5 Try to encourage narrow stretched, wide, tucked, piked and straddle positions in flight. |
| Group 6: Practise straddle forward roll and then take the roll into a balance. | 6 The balance may be the result of a sideways action. It does not just have to continue forward. |

**Final activity**

Apparatus away.
Stand well.

*Note*: You may wish to replace one of the group activities with continued *headstand* practice.

# YEAR 4

**Autumn Term:** **TRAVELLING**
**Session 7:** **Achieving variety using body shape emphasis**

Explain to the children the intention of this work. Then they will be able to apply the principles to other aspects. (See *Achieving Variety*).

|  | Content | Teaching points |
|---|---|---|
| **Warm up** | 1 Run softly around the hall — on command sprint on spot. Repeat. | 1 Flexible ankles, head up — conscious emphasis on speed change. |
|  | 2 Repeat but now with long steps for travelling and very small steps on spot. | 2 Drive hard off back leg reaching forward with the other. Precision of small steps. |
| **Body preparation** | 1 Standing, ankle springing leading to skip jumping (bouncing). | 1 Do not move to bouncing too soon. |
|  | 2 Kneeling hands on ground, circling alternate legs. | 2 ⎫ |
|  | 3 Lie on back, knees bent, arms by side alternately raise arms above head to touch floor. | 3 ⎬ Slow pressure to ensure good mobility. |
| **Floor activities** | 1 Being on shoulders, rock or roll to arrive on seat. | |
|  | 2 Begin similarly and move to arrive on different body part/s. | 2 Emphasize clear held starting and finishing positions. Pick out children's ideas. |
|  | 3 Arrive on seat (as in 1) in tucked position/extended position/emphasizing one side of hips/legs apart/legs together, etc. | 3 All these are possible variations. Singly or in combination they offer many opportunities for variety. |

| Content | Teaching points |
|---|---|
| 4 Practise 3 jumps from 2 feet to 2 feet. Repeat. | 4 Landing of one jump to lead directly into take off of next. |
| 5 Experiment with these keeping legs tightly together. | 5 'Squeeze' legs tightly together. |
| 6 Repeat with legs apart. | 6 Astride or split forwards and back. |
| 7 Repeat with legs bent or legs straight. | 7 Tucked jumps require quick leg extension — prior to landing. |
| 8 Repeat 1st jump legs together and stretched, 2nd jump legs apart and stretched, 3rd jump free choice. | 8 Ensure correct interpretation of these variations. |
| 9 Repeat: Child's own choice. *Note*; Develop this with other kinds of jump (not 2.2). | 9 Children consciously choose variation. Ask them to articulate (in words) their choices. |

**Final activity**

Lie on tummy, keep feet still and come to standing.

Then:
Stand well.

Arm strengthening task.

# YEAR 4

**Autumn Term:** TRAVELLING AND BALANCE
**Session 8:** Achieving variety using speed emphasis

| | Content | Teaching points |
|---|---|---|
| **Warm up** | 1 Gentle bouncing on spot, gradually increasing height. | 1 Full extension through legs. Relaxed neck. Arms assisting to get lift. |
| | 2 3 runs on spot followed by 3 bounding leaps. | 2 Feel difference when the back leg drives for the bounding leap. |
| | 3 Run a few steps, spring, land and spring straight *up* again. | 3 Only a short run is necessary. Extend legs and feet ready for landing. Emphasize the '*up again*'. |
| **Floor activities** | 1 Make up an *action phrase* to include<br>A balance<br>A jump<br>A roll<br>A hands/feet action<br>Practise it until it is correct. | 1 Children experiment a) with different kinds of action b) with different ways of ordering the actions. Remind the children of the term *Action phrase*. |
| | 2 Use your action phrase and see if you can make some parts fast and some parts slow. | 2 *Vital* that children identify the *natural* speed of some actions (*e.g.* jump = fast: arriving at balance = slow). Discuss this — and identify those actions whose speed *can* be changed. |
| | 3 All practise your hands/feet action. Highlight the speed you have selected. Ditto the roll. (Also repeat with jump and balance if necessary). | 3 Preparation is important. Tension crucial in order not to collapse in slow actions. |

| **Content** | **Teaching points** |
|---|---|
| 4  Put whole back together again. | 4  Emphasize clarity and control. Demand a good finished product. |

**Final activity**

| | |
|---|---|
| In pairs, controlled follow my leader. Squat jumping. Change leader.<br><br>Then:<br>Stand well. | Leg strengthener. |

# YEAR 4

**TRAVELLING AND BALANCE**
**Achieving variety using space emphasis**

|  | **Content** | **Teaching points** |
|---|---|---|
| **Warm up** | 1 Run softly around the hall — on command sprint on spot. Repeat. | 1 Flexible ankles, head up — conscious emphasis on speed change. |
|  | 2 Repeat but now with long steps travelling and very small steps on spot. | 2 Drive hard off back leg reaching forward with the other. Precision of small steps. |
|  | 3 Repeat, two feet to two feet, zig-zagging in travelling, tucking knees up to chest on spot. | 3 Explosive tension to push off into jumps. Let hips help to achieve zig-zag effect. Keep head up in tucked jumps — stretching legs quickly before landing. |
| **Body preparation** | 1 Squat, 1 leg bent and 1 straight — quickly change legs (bear dancing). | 1 5 × first but increasing as appropriate. |
|  | 2 Lie on front, hands behind back and raise chest × 5. | 2 Held raised position for a count of 3. Press toes down. |
|  | 3 Straddle sit, press tummy to floor. | 3 Slow pressure. |

|  | **Content** | **Teaching points** |
|---|---|---|

## Apparatus activities

6 Groups<br>3 groups with a bench: 3 groups with 2 mats

TASKS FOR BENCH GROUPS
1 Either begin *on* or *away from* bench in a balance. Move away from or towards on a zig-zag path-way — at each change of direction show a clear balance.

1 Vary the travel between balances. Vary the balance.

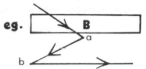

TASK FOR MAT GROUPS
2 Travel continuously across the mat finding ways of having legs high in the air or close to the mat.

2 You should see jumps, rolls, wheeling actions, leaping, etc.

Change over groups and repeat tasks

## Final activity

Mat group: lean against climbing frame.
Bench group: lean against benches.
Bend and straighten arms 6 times.

Arm strengthener.

Apparatus away.<br>Stand well.

# YEAR 4

**Autumn Term:** **BALANCE**
**Session 10:** **Introducing handstand**

| | Content | Teaching points |
|---|---|---|
| **Warm up** | 1 On commands alternate running with bouncing on the spot. | 1 Feel the difference in the two actions — forward movement changing precisely to upward movement. |
| **Body preparation** | 1 Increase height of bouncing on spot, with final jump having a tucked body shape. | 1 Greater flexion needed for increased height. Rapid tucking of knees to chest (not head down) and opening out prior to landing. |
| | 2 Practise feet/hands/feet travelling (catsprings). | 2 Work hard on arms and legs. Feel weight is taken on arms before feet touch down. |
| | 3 Sitting, legs straight out in front. Gently push trunk down to legs. Push, push and push and relax. Repeat 4 times. | 3 Importance of easy pressure not sudden force. |

**Floor activities**

As a class activity practise the preparatory stages 1 and 2 of the handstand. (See *Specific Skills Guide* — Handstand).

*Then:*

| | |
|---|---|
| 1 Push off bent leg swinging other leg *straight* up. | 1 Head looking forward. Fingers spread — hands shoulder width apart — elbow locked. This is in effect the 'end' of the lunge step. |
| 2 As above but the push off leg swings into air as the other leg comes to the ground. | 2 Feeling of legs changing places in the air. Legs straight. |

*Note:* Some (only a few!) children may need to remain at this stage. Most should now move on to stages 3, 4 and 5 for the handstand as on page 171.

| Content | Teaching points |
|---|---|
| Then continue with: | |
| 1 Take a few steps jump and land. | 1 One footed take off, two footed landing. Ensure neat and safe landing. |
| 2 Repeat with greater energy (not more steps) to gain more height. | 2 Identify use of arms to assist in life. No tension in neck. Explosive take-off action. Clear, exact landings. |
| 3 Repeat with *landing* action being the preparation for a hands/feet movement. | 3 Develop rhythmic pattern. |
| 4 Repeat making pattern travel along a straight line. | 4 Twist body in first action, keep continuity going from first action into the 2 springing actions. |

**Final activity**  Lie on stomach raise head and heels quickly 5 times. Stand well.

*Note*: Handstand practice is best suited to group work after this introductory stage. It can, of course, be a task the whole class attempts for very short periods at any time in the body preparation section. Support children (see page 172) if they will benefit.

# YEAR 4

The children should now be able to do the following skills.

1 1 Jump (knowing difference between 1 footed and 2 footed take off) — Jump with a turn — use hurdle step.
  2 Forward and backward roll.
  3 Headstand.
  4 Handstand (beginnings).

2 Know how to vary movement.
  a with changing body shape
  b with changing speed
  c with changing pathways.

3 Make up simple action phrases.

The next sessions therefore should make good any noted weaknesses in these aspects.

Any aspects particularly enjoyed by the children should be repeated.

**For your notes and comments:**

# YEAR 4

**Spring Term:** **TRAVELLING AND BALANCE**
**Session 1:** **Adding variety to action phrases**

|  | Content | Teaching points |
|---|---|---|
| **Warm up** | 1 Soft running. On commands 'left' touch floor with left hand, 'right' with right hand, 'squat' both hands and 'jump', jump. | 1 Running in and out of each other — after each action continue running. Action must be crisp and purposeful — jump fully extended. |
|  | 2 Travel using jumping, rolling and moving on hands and feet consciously curling, arching, twisting and stretching the spine. | 2 May need articulation by the teacher. Expect high leaps, tucked rolls, cartwheeling actions twisting jumps etc. Active spine work. |
| **Body preparation** | 1 Front support on hands, walk arms round feet. | 1 Keep feet fixed. |
|  | 2 Practise press ups from kneeling. | 2 5 ×, then 6 × etc. Take the weight *just above* the knees. |
|  | 3 Sitting, legs in front, stroke inside of one leg with sole of foot of other leg. | 3 Ensure good hip mobility. |
| **Floor activities** | 1 Practise handstands. | 1 (See *Specific Skills Guide* — Handstand.) Emphasis now on lunge step preparation. Tension essential. |
|  | 2 Repeat, and when feet touch down take it straight into a jump and landing. | 2 Prepare mentally for the second part of the phrase. |

| Content | Teaching points |
|---|---|
| 3 When (2) is fluent add *another* action to the pattern. | 3 Allow children to get (2) right before moving on. The next action must flow on from the landing of the jump. |
| 4 Now add variety to this pattern by thinking about changing body shape. | 4 Try to encourage the children to experiment freely before arriving at finished pattern. |
| 5 Practise each part in turn trying different possibilities. | 5 This will encourage clarity. |
| 6 Return to finished action phrase. | 6 Identify how different shapes have changed what at the start were quite similar phrases. |

**Final activity**

| | |
|---|---|
| 1 Trying to turn partner over — partner resisting.<br><br>Then:<br>Stand well. | 1 Tension throughout body needed. |

# YEAR 4

**Spring Term:** **TRAVELLING AND BALANCE**
**Session 2:** **Adding variety to action phrases**

| | Content | Teaching points |
|---|---|---|
| **Warm up** | 1 Free running. | 1 Emphasize one aspect of running (See *Specific Skills Guide* — Running.). |
| | 2 Short run, hurdle step, jump and land. | 2 The 'hurdle' is the preparation for the strong double footed take off into the spring. |
| **Body preparation** | a) Happy cat/angry cat. | a) Hold each position before relaxing. |
| | b) Kneel sitting back on heels, circle arms backwards. | b) A push not a swing. |
| | c) On all fours gently move body forward over arms. | c) Hands flat — easy pressure. |
| **Floor activities** | 1 Practise handstands as in Session 1. | 1 Feel the tension prior to, and during the action. Squeeze legs together when inverted. |
| | 2 Repeat and try to put your feet down in a different finishing position. | 2 Expect twisting and arching actions. For this to happen think *ahead*. |
| | 3 Repeat 2 and then use steps to take you into a good position for another handstand. Do another handstand. | 3 Adjustment mid-phrase will need to be clarified. Handstand — touchdown — adjust with steps — handstand. |
| | 4 Now somewhere add a quite different balance to this pattern of two handstands. | 4 Encourage the children to play with ideas. Different starts? Different finishes? Can it be in the middle of the phrase? |

## Content

5  Do whole phrase TWICE but
   changing the floor pattern.

## Teaching points

5  Children may have to adjust
   actions. Ask them what the
   floor pattern is (Is it a curve,
   zig-zag, straight line?).

**Final activity**   Stand well.

# YEAR 4

**REVISION**
**Revision of basic skills clarifying the body shape of the actions**

|  | **Content** | **Teaching points** |
|---|---|---|
| **Warm up** | 1 Running softly with jumping and landing. | 1 Use the space well — allow runs to be a purposeful preparation for the jump. |
| **Body preparation** | 1 a) Sitting legs forward. Rotate ankles.<br>b) Press trunk down onto legs: 3 presses and relax. | 1 a) Encourage maximum flexibility.<br>b) Not a forcing action. |
|  | 2 Lie on back, knees bent, arch body to take weight on feet and shoulders. | 2 Keep feet firmly on the floor and try not to slide. |

**Apparatus activities**

6 Groups
Specific tasks for each different group

| | |
|---|---|
| Group 1: a) Begin on floor: forward roll into a handstand.<br>b) Begin on bench and forward roll down bench into handstand. | 1 a) Control legs carefully as you and rotate. Prepare feet for stepping (lunge) into handstand.<br>b) For the more able children only. (Another mat may be needed on top of bench). |
| Group 2: Practise forward rolls along the top of the box beginning on the floor. | 2 Grip sides of box, push from feet to raise hips. |
| Group 3: Begin *on* bench gripping sides with hands. Push, as in beginning of handstand and twist feet to land on floor. | 3 As confidence increases gradually get legs higher. NB. this *must* be controlled by strong grip of hands on bench. Head looking forward initially. |

| Content | Teaching points |
|---|---|
| Group 4: Practise headstands. Find ways of putting an action before or after the headstand. | 4 (See *Specific Skills Guide* — Headstand.) Children need to think hard about the way they can link an action to a headstand. |
| Group 5: Jump from bench with $\frac{1}{2}$ turn, land in control and then move into a backward roll. | 5 Control essential in linking landing to backward roll. |
| Group 6: Practise moving from feet to hands to feet. Hands only on mat. | 6 Feet begin on one side of the mat and finish on the other therefore there is likely to be a twist during the action. |

For each group emphasize the clarity of body shape within the action.

Where relevant ask the children to vary their movements by changing the body shape in some way.

*Note*: Task cards may be helpful here.

## Final activity

Apparatus away.
Stand well.

## Apparatus pattern

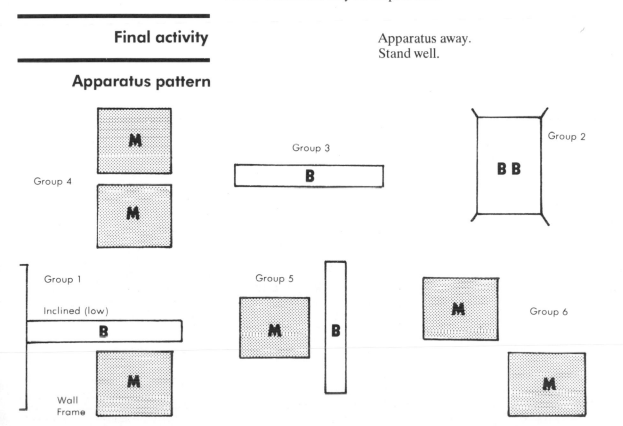

79

# YEAR 4

**Spring Term:** **SPRINGING AND LANDING**
**Sessions 5 and 6:** **On to and from the apparatus**

| | Content | Teaching points |
|---|---|---|
| **Warm up** | 1 Jogging, alternating with (a) Tuck Jump; (b) Star Jump; (c) Turning Jump. | 1 Call out '(a), (b) or (c)'. Emphasize quality of jump — into Jogging again. |
| **Body preparation** | 1 Squat thrusts × 10. | 1 Or as many as is appropriate. |
| | 2 Foot circling. | 2 All directions. |
| | 3 Take weight on hands and push back to feet. | 3 'Give' in the arms a little, followed by explosive *push*. |
| **Apparatus activities** | General tasks for all apparatus. | |
| | 1 Find places on the apparatus where you can push off from hands to land on the floor. | 1 Encourage children to try different appropriate places. Legs need to thrust out as arms push. Children should start in squat position. |
| | 2 Approach run *on to* part of the apparatus; jump high into the air and land in control. Vary the body shape in the jump. | 2 Intention is for a continuous action. Landing area must be quite clear. |
| | 3 Cross any part of the apparatus just touching with hands trying to push and have a moment of flight. | 3 Arms need to 'give' prior to the final push — rest of body similarly, a recoil and an explosive thrust. |

|  | **Content** | **Teaching points** |
| --- | --- | --- |

4 Make a pattern of springing and jumping which moves from floor to apparatus several times.

4 Remind children of the different activities already practised. Give them time for this. Encourage good use of *floor*.

*Note*: Give these tasks separately to *ALL* groups.

**Final activity**  Put benches to floor. Place feet under benches (*knees bent*) bring head to knees rapidly 10 times.

Stomach strengthener. (Vital that knees are bent.)

Apparatus away.
Stand well.

## Apparatus pattern

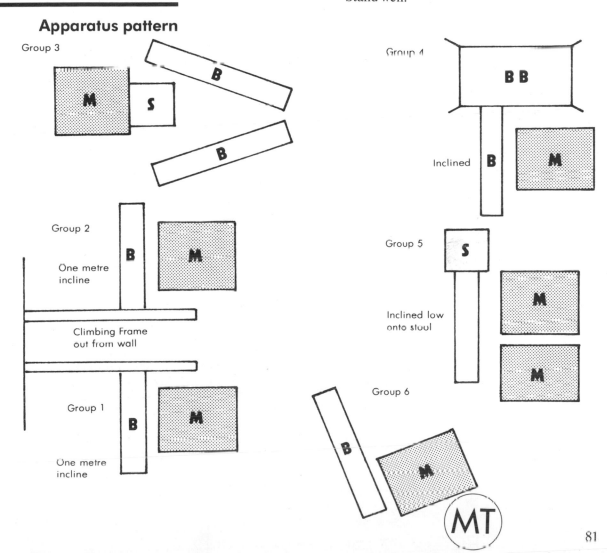

Group 3

Group 4

Group 2

One metre incline

Climbing Frame out from wall

Group 1

One metre incline

Inclined

Group 5

Inclined low onto stool

Group 6

# YEAR 4

**Spring Term:** **ROTATION**
**Session 7:** **Turning actions**

| | Content | Teaching points |
|---|---|---|
| **Warm up** | 1 Travel over the floor bouncing from 2 feet to 2 feet. | 1 Clear directional changes. Landing of one action = preparation for next. |
| | 2 Alternate bouncing similarly *on spot* with side slipping action. | 2 Feel different emphasis of 2 feet together, then alternate legs. |
| **Body preparation** | 1 Practise taking weight on hands, or practise handstands. | 1 (See *Specific Skills Guide* — Handstand). Remind of appropriate safety points. |
| | 2 Stand sideways, hand on wall. Swing leg forward and back trying to touch head on back swing with foot. Change legs. | 2 Try not to bend trunk. |
| **Floor activities** | 1 Move over the floor travelling and turning. | 1 Articulate the varied responses shown by the children. |
| | 2 Repeat, clearly changing your turning action as you go. | 2 Verbal commands to change may help here. |
| | 3 Show a pattern of pivot turn, into jumping turn, into rolling turn. | 3 Repeat several times to ensure variety of response and *accurate* response. |
| | 4 Revise 5 basic jumps. | 4 (*i.e.* 2 feet to 2 feet. 1 to 2 etc.) |
| | 5 Select 3 of these jumps and make them turn. | 5 (See *Specific Skills Guide* — Jumping). |

| Content | Teaching points |
|---|---|
| 6 Now think of an action which does not turn and make it part of the pattern practised in 5. | 6 Begin to discuss with the children what is a turn. Try balancing, travelling, hands/feet actions for non-turning movements. Do they turn at all? Partly? |
| 7 Put together an ACTION PHRASE which has 2 turning actions and 1 which does not turn. | 7 The ideas for this will have been developed in the earlier tasks (1–6). |

**Final activity**

| | |
|---|---|
| In pairs squat jumping follow my leader. Change role.

Then:
Stand well. | Leg strengthener. |

# YEAR 4

**Spring Term:** **ROTATION**
**Session 8:** **Different kinds of turning action**

|  | Content | Teaching points |
|---|---|---|
| **Warm up** | 1 Running softly with jumping and landing. | 1 Good use of space … controlled jumping *up* from the run. |
| **Body preparation** | 1 Practise handstands. | 1 Children should now be confident in this activity therefore expect tension and stretching. |
|  | 2 Stand and kick the hand held at shoulder height in various directions. | 2 Encourage children to push just a little further each time. |
| **Floor activities** | 1 Revise turning jumps from last lesson. |  |
|  | 2 Practise the turning jumps taking off from one foot. Swing free leg and arms to assist the turn. Land on two feet. | 2 Step on to the take off leg to gain momentum. |
|  | 3 Contrast this with a turning jump taking off from two feet. | 3 (See *Specific Skills Guide* — Jumping.) |
|  | 4 Step on to one foot and pivot on that foot. | 4 Use step to initiate pivot, other leg and arms then assist. |
|  | 5 Step → pivot → step → turning jump. | 5 Move out of pivot before it loses its momentum and straight into jump. Discuss the notion of axes. (See Section 2 units — Rotation). |

| Content | Teaching points |
|---|---|
| 6 Practise 2 pivoting turns using different parts of the body. Try to travel between the two. | 6 Expect use of knees, seat, feet. (If on stomach or back, axis is different — *may* warrant explanation) — clear *action* to cross the floor into second pivot. |
| 7 Try turning now by a wheeling action (the body looking and feeling like a wheel — arms and legs = SPOKES). | 7 Suggest moving from feet to hands to feet to help this feeling. Try 'spokes of wheel' idea. (Discuss axis — medial). |
| 8 Put together a phrase which includes: — a wheeling turn, a jumping turn, a pivoting turn, and an action which does not turn. | 8 The non-turning action need *not* come at the end of the phrase. |

**Final activity**

Take up press up position. Try to clap hands, quickly replacing hands on floor.

Then:
Stand well.

Stomach/Arm strengthener.

# YEAR 4

**Spring Term:** **ROTATION**
**Session 9:** **Introducing cartwheel**

| | Content | Teaching points |
|---|---|---|
| **Warm up** | 1 On commands alternate running with bouncing on the spot. | 1 Feel the difference in the two actions — forward movement changing precisely to upward movement. |
| **Body preparation** | 1 Increase height of bouncing on spot, with final jump having a tucked body shape. | 1 Greater flexion needed for increased height. Rapid tucking of knees to chest (not head down) and opening out prior to landing. |
| | 2 Lie on back, raise both legs part and close legs × 5. | 2 Hold strong tension. (Push small of back flat to the floor.) |
| | 3 Practise handstands. | 3 Remind and reinforce preparatory position, use of lunge leg, tension in stomach and legs. |
| **Floor activities** | 1 Teach cartwheel. | 1 (See *Specific Skills Guide* — Cartwheel.) |

**Apparatus activities**

*Four Groups*

*Specific tasks for each group*

Group 1: Continue to practise cartwheel.

1 Teacher remain at this station.

Group 2: Practise forward and backward rolls. (2 mats).

2 Ask children to find out whilst they are working what makes this kind of turn different from other turns practised.

| Content | Teaching points |
|---|---|
| Group 3: Practise run, hurdle step, jump onto bench, immediate turning, jump off. | 3 Do not anticipate the turn prior to take off. (No 360° turns) |
| Group 4: 2 × 2 mats lengthwise. Make a pattern of 3 turning actions which travel along the length of the mats. Try different ideas. | 4 Remind children of the different actions already experienced. |

Inevitably there will be some queuing in this session.

## Final activity

Apparatus away.
Stand well.

## Apparatus pattern

Group 1

No apparatus needed

Group 2

B | M

Group 3

B | M

Group 4

# YEAR 4

**Spring Term:** **ROTATION**
**Session 10:** **Emphasizing different kinds of turning action**

| | Content | Teaching points |
|---|---|---|
| **Warm up** | 1 Travel using jumping, rolling and moving on hands and feet, consciously curling, arching, twisting and stretching the spine. | 1 Active spine work. (See Session 1 this term). |
| **Body preparation** | 1 Lie on back, knees bent, raise trunk up to sitting and lower. | 1 No collapse as body lowers. |
| | 2 a) foot circling<br> b) standing-hip circling<br> c) straddle sitting, press tummy to floor. | 2 (a, b, and c) Slow deliberate pressure. |

**Apparatus activities**

Use all mats evenly spaced. Children in groups.

*General tasks for ALL groups*

| Content | Teaching points |
|---|---|
| 1 Revise forward roll and backward roll. | 1 In order to clarify the notion of the *lateral* axis. |
| 2 Find another kind of roll which does not turn around this axis. | 2 Long roll will probably be shown or barrel roll. |
| 3 Show a rolling turn which finishes<br>a) with a jumping turn and then<br>b) with a wheeling turn. | 3 Can the children explain the differences? |

| Content | Teaching points |
|---|---|
| 4 Begin away from mat with back to it *not* on feet. Use a turn to face this mat, another to travel towards it and another to cross it. | 4 Articulate the various possibilities *e.g.* pivoting turn to face mat (which parts?) — wheeling turn to approach — jumping turn to cross (what kind of jump?) |
| 5 Approach, cross and leave your mat using turning actions to include: jumping, rolling, wheeling and pivoting. | 5 Remind of previous work. |

Children can practise parts on the floor whilst waiting for their turn wherever possible.

**Final activity**

Lie on back, raise left leg a little way, hold for 5 and lower. Repeat with right leg. Repeat again.

Stomach strengthener.

Mats away.
Stand well.

# YEAR 4

## Spring Term: Assessment and consolidation sessions

The children should now be showing some competence in: and knowledge of:

1 Basic skills (forward/backward roll, handstand, headstand, jumping/landing, cartwheel).
   and should understand how they can be
   a) linked together in action phrases
   b) varied
   c) used to illustrate the movement units (*e.g.* cartwheel … rotation).

2 Springing actions from feet to feet, and feet to hands to feet.

3 Turning and travelling.

4 Additionally, they should be *appreciating good* movement.

Use these sessions to revise or reinforce any of these aspects.

As before, do repeat elements which have been particularly enjoyed.

**For your notes and comments:**

# YEAR 5

**Autumn Term:** **PARTNER WORK**
**Session 1:** **Following pathways emphasizing clear body shape within the action**

| | Content | Teaching points |
|---|---|---|
| **Warm up** | 1 Free running with change of direction. | 1 Emphasize mobility in changing direction. Precise and clear steps. |
| **Body preparation** | 1 Circle both arms in front of body<br>a) both in same direction<br>b) in opposite directions inwards<br>c) in opposite directions outwards | 1 Push, not swing. |
| | 2 In pairs: face partners, arms held out straight, one partner's palms on back of others. One tries to push up while other resists. | 2 Repeat × 2 or more appropriate. |
| | 3 Practise taking weight on hands, and then practise handstands (individually). | 3 Consistent emphasis now on good quality (∴ tension and stretching). |
| **Floor activities** | 1 Use the words springing, rolling, sliding and stepping on to hands, make a *ZIG ZAG* pathway action phrase. Repeat. | 1 Make the ends of each straight line clear. If necessary practise the direction changes in isolation. Repetition essential for clarity. |
| | 2 Try to trace a *curved* pathway where you stay constantly in contact with the floor. Repeat. | 2 Difficult — concentration needed. Quality still essential. Clear body shape throughout. |

| Content | Teaching points |
|---|---|
| 3 *TWO's* with a partner make up a 'following' sequence using zig zag and curved pathways. Use ideas practised in tasks 1 and 2. | 3 Concentrate on quality again. Extended leg — strong/ controlled springing — good body shape. |

**Final activity**

| | |
|---|---|
| As a class squat jump 3 forward, 3 to the left, 3 to the right, 3 backwards.<br><br>Then:<br>Stand well. | Do this rhythmically in order to assist children. |

# YEAR 5

**PARTNER WORK**
**Following pathways, emphasizing travelling towards, away from etc. low apparatus**

|  | Content | Teaching points |
|---|---|---|
| **Warm up** | 1 Running in and out of class gently. | 1 Good body carriage, flexible ankles. |
|  | 2 Repeat, adding jumps with $\frac{1}{2}$ turn. Good landing. | 2 Short runs to develop power for good take off. Use arms correctly in the turn. |
| **Body preparation** | 1 In pairs, lie on front, try to raise heels as partner resists. | 1 Change role × 2. |
|  | 2 Individually, caterpillar walk. | 2 Keep hand fixed and legs straight. |
|  | 3 Lie on stomach, grip ankles and try to straighten legs. | 3 Easy pressure. |
| **Apparatus activities** | *Benches and mats*: use all available and also box tops or low nesting table | |
|  | With a partner. | |
|  | 1 Follow your partner's pathway towards, on to, across, along, away from etc. the apparatus. | 1 Remind of various actions possible. Try to encourage children not to stay too close to the apparatus. |
|  | 2 Change role. | |
|  | 3 Trace a pathway in the shape of a W. A goes first B follows. (Use apparatus as in 1 and 2). | 3 Where will it begin? (on or away from?). It must keep coming back to that place, but further along. |

| Content | Teaching points |
|---|---|
| 4 With B leading — similarly in D shaped pathway. | 4 Does it cross the apparatus? Do you ever touch the apparatus? Try several possibilities — don't just take the first idea. |
| 5 Children select an appropriate letter and devise a 'following' sequence using words towards, away from, along, etc. (the bench). | 5 Articulate the good ideas to the class. Use mat effectively also. |

**Final activity**

Trunk curls tucking feet under the apparatus (10 times).

Knees bent.
Stomach strengthener.

Apparatus away.
Stand well.

# YEAR 5

| | | |
|---|---|---|
| **Autumn Term:** | **PARTNER WORK** | |
| **Session 3:** | **Contrasting body shape in 'following' action phrases** | |

| | **Content** | **Teaching points** |
|---|---|---|
| **Warm up** | 1 On command 'A' jog; on 'B' bounce on the spot; on 'C' side slip. | 1 Accurate, controlled — good springy feel. |
| **Body preparation** | 1 Lie on back, clasp hands and try to pass legs through hands to behind head. | |
| | 2 Stand, stretch alternate arms upwards. | |
| | 3 Practise taking weight on hands in different ways. Then practise handstands/ cartwheels. | 3 Show various examples. Then more specifically show correct handstands/cartwheels. |
| **Floor activities** | 1 *Individually* devise an action phrase showing 4 *different* actions which show changes in body shape. | 1 Example: spread cartwheel into stretched catspring, into tucked jump, into stretched handstand. Discuss with the children possible parts of the phrase — do not, if possible, give an example of the whole phrase. |
| | 2 In pairs A shows his phrase to B. (Or vice versa). Identify the actions (*e.g.* jump, handstand, etc.) and B try the phrase but *not* with the same body shape. Take each part in turn and try ideas. | 2 The idea is that children do not have to match exactly the partners' work. Modifications are possible if body shape can be changed. (*e.g.* A handstand can become a bunny jump). |

|  | **Content** | **Teaching points** |
|---|---|---|
| | 3 A practises his phrase.<br>  B practises his phrase. | 3 Trying to perfect clarity of<br>  shape. |
| | 4 A does a movement, then 'B'<br>  docs his first movement, then<br>  'A' does his second, etc. | |

**Final activity**  Duck fighting.

Then:
Stand well.

(See Year 3 Spring Term Session 3.)

# YEAR 5

**Autumn Term:** **ROTATION**
**Session 4:** **Turning into and out of balance**

|  | Content | Teaching points |
|---|---|---|
| **Warm up** | 1 Soft running. On commands 'left' touch floor with left hand, 'right' right hand, 'squat' both hands and 'jump' jump. | 1 Running in and out of each other — after each action continue running. Action must be crisp and purposeful — jump fully extended. |
|  | 2 Travel using springing, rolling and stepping on hands and feet consciously curling, arching, twisting and stretching the spine. | 2 May need articulation by the teacher. Expect high leaps into tucked rolls, spread cartwheeling actions twisting jumps etc. Active spine work. |
| **Body preparation** | 1 Kneel, sit on heels swing one arm upwards and the other downwards and backwards. Change arms. | 1 Feel the moment where more 'push' can be given. |
|  | 2 Kneel, hands on floor, move forward over arms. | 2 For wrist mobility. |
|  | 3 Straddle sit and press tummy to floor. | 3 Push legs a little wider now. |
|  | 4 Practise handstands and cartwheels. | 4 Emphasize 'lunge' step. |

| | Content | Teaching points |
|---|---|---|
| **Floor activities** | 1 Develop a pattern of: balance → travel → balance → travel → balance. | 1 Emphasize equally the different elements. Call out the different kinds of movements the children are showing. |
| | 2 Revise and reinforce:<br>a) what balance means<br>b) kinds of balance<br>c) emphasize the point of moving 'off' balance. | 2 See Years 3 and 4. Small/large parts: single parts: two parts: parts on same side of body opposite side: rounded parts etc. |
| | 3 Repeat pattern (1) making held moments of balance clearer. | 3 Is there a 'perched' feeling? Are balances varied? Do they really challenge the child? |
| | 4 Repeat: changing the travelling actions into TURNING actions and emphasizing the moment of going off balance. | 4 Revise and reinforce the different kinds of turning action. Jumping and pivoting, wheeling, rolling turns. Try each out in turn if necessary. |

*Note*: Spend time on task 2 in order to reinforce the importance of knowing the point of going 'off' balance.

| | | |
|---|---|---|
| **Final activity** | In pairs, A tries to turn B over whilst B resists. | General body tension. |

# YEAR 5

**Autumn Term:** **ROTATION**
**Session 5:** **Turning into and out of balance**

|  | Content | Teaching points |
|---|---|---|
| **Warm up** | 1 Running, zig-zagging with rapid changes of direction. | 1 Precise clear changes — good spacing. |
|  | 2 Run, jump and land freely. | 2 Upward action after landing important for continuity. |
| **Body preparation** | 1 Practise ways of moving from feet to hands to feet. | 1 Try to get hips high and prepare feet for landing. Work hard. |
|  | 2 Kneeling, walk hands as far round as possible to alternate sides. | 2 Feel strong twist in trunk. |
|  | 3 Kneeling, hands on ground, circling alternate legs. | 3 Do this quite slowly to stretch as far as possible. |
| **Floor activities** | 1 Revise your pattern of balance — turn — balance — turn — balance from last session. | 1 Try to encourage clarity of action and point out the differences shown. |
|  | 2 Explore possibilities of turning jumps into balance. | 2 Either the landing itself becoming the balance, or use the landing to transfer weight into a different balance. |
|  | 3 Try same turning jump twice, but finishing in a different balance position each time. | 3 Select an example to illustrate this clearly. |
|  | 4 Practise a pattern where you turn and jump *into* a balance move 'off' balance into a roll. | |

| Content | Teaching points |
|---|---|
| 5  Having examined turning jumps into balance, try other kinds of turning action to take you into balance.<br>a) rolling — balance —<br>b) pivoting<br>c) wheeling. | 5  Select carefully here. Remind of axes again. Verbal commands may help *e.g.* 'Ready balanced? Roll and turn into balance (hold!) Pivot into balance (come to feet!) Turning jump into balance and cartwheel into final balance'. |

**Final activity**

| | |
|---|---|
| Take weight on hands and push to come back to feet. Repeat several times.<br><br>Then:<br>Stand well. | Feel weight is on arms before the 'give' and thrust. |

# YEAR 5

**Autumn Term:** **ROTATION**
**Session 6:** **Turning into and out of balance on low apparatus**

|  | Content | Teaching points |
|---|---|---|
| **Warm up** | 1 Short run, hurdle step, jump and land. | 1 Use 'hurdle' as a preparation for the strong double footed take off into the jump. |
| **Body preparation** | 1 Hopping alternate legs × 10. | 1 Keep top half of body erect. |
|  | 2 Take weight on hands and place feet in a different landing position. Repeat several times. | 2 Twist in trunk is important here. |
|  | 3 Straddle sit, rock back to shoulders and press legs wider apart. | 3 Press inside of thighs — keep legs stretched. |

**Apparatus activities**

Benches/low nesting tables/box tops and mats (Space out evenly in hall)

*General tasks for all groups*

| Content | Teaching points |
|---|---|
| 1 Revise balancing: <br> a) wholly on bench <br> b) partly on bench and floor. | 1 Bench can be grasped, pushed against, pulled against to maintain balance. |
| 2 Similarly practise inverted balances. | 2 Easier than on the floor because child can grip, etc. |
| 3 Don't forget tasks 1 and 2. Now find turning actions to: <br> a) cross the bench <br> b) take you along the bench. | 3 Again, remind of the various possibilities. |
| 4 Cross the bench with turning jumps: <br> a) not touching it <br> b) making one contact. | 4 Essential to get good preparatory action here to assist in clearing bench. emphasize good style. |

102

| Content | Teaching points |
|---|---|
| 5  Turning jump on to bench, pause, turning jump off. | 5  Precise held moment, prepare and push off for second turning jump. |
| 6  Cross bench with a turn putting hands on the bench. | 6  Placement of hands — grip bench, lock elbows, swing legs high. Repeat several times. |
| 7  Repeat with one hand on the bench and one on floor on opposite side. | 7  Reach forward into this action, turn hands sideways. Ask: what axis are you turning about? |
| 8  Cross bench as in 6 or 7 and return with a turning jump. | 8  How does the turning jump differ from the previous action (axis-wise)? |
| 9  Repeat but begin with a balance, hold balance at end of first action and end of second action. | 9  Is the balance appropriate for the next action? If not there must be a transition (linking action-explain this word). |
| 10  Roll across mat to finish with inverted balance on bench (or floor and bench). Repeat and show a different answer to this task. | 10  Axis here? If forwards/backwards roll? If sideways roll? |

**Final activity**  Lean against benches. Bend and straighten arms 10 times.  Arms/stomach strengthener.

*Note*:  this session has many tasks and so will probably require additional time devoted to it.

Then:
Stand well.

# YEAR 5

**SPRINGING AND LANDING**
**Introducing 'Round-Off'**

| | Content | Teaching points |
|---|---|---|
| **Warm up** | 1 Free running, changing direction constantly. | 1 A controlled purposeful action — general space awareness. |
| **Body preparation** | 1 Straddle sit, rock on to back and press thighs outwards. | 1 Gentle pressure to encourage 'splits' position. |
| | 2 Remain in straddle position, press trunk over left leg, to centre, over right leg and sit straight. Repeat 4 times. | 2 Again press not force. Keeping legs stretched. |
| | 3 Front support position, try to clap hands, quickly replacing hands on floor. | 3 Try more than one clap if appropriate. |
| **Floor activities** | 1 Revise travelling along a straight line from feet to hands to feet. | 1 Prepare correctly (lunge step) — work hard on arms to hold hips high and prepare feet for landing. Twist needed to maintain straight line. |
| | 2 Revise cartwheels. | 2 (See *Specific Skills Guide* — Cartwheel.) |
| | 3 Repeat, but at top of cartwheel bring legs sharply together (stretched), twist hips to land facing your starting position. | 3 This is a way to achieve a 'round off'. Select a clear example to clarify this. Child will now be facing the direction from which he started. Check new hands position — *Specific Skills Guide* — Round-off. |

| Content | Teaching points |
|---|---|
| 4 *When ready*, from a short approach run skip step into the round off. | 4 Organize this so that those children ready for this, all work towards the same direction. Those not ready continue practising task 3. |
| 5 Make up a pattern of 3 springing/jumping actions to include if possible the round off. | 5 Most children will manage a form of this. Try to encourage fluency as one jump/spring leads into the next. |

**Final activity**

Lie flat on back — stretch and tense body — relax. Stand.

Then:
Stand well.

Children should be able to hold tension in this way by now.

# YEAR 5

**Autumn Term:** **SPRINGING AND LANDING**
**Sessions 8, 9 and 10:** **Hurdle step to spring board, springing off and on to ropes**

| | Content | Teaching points |
|---|---|---|
| **Warm up** | 1 Run, jump with $\frac{1}{2}$ turn, land. Repeat several times. | 1 Correct arm action in the turn. Spring up before continuing to run. |
| **Body preparation** | 1 a) Squat, 1 leg bent the other straight — quick changes of legs. <br> b) Kneel, sitting back on heels, arms circling backwards. | 1 a) Keep back straight <br><br> b) Press a little further each time. |
| | 2 Practise handstand, cartwheel, round off, etc. | 2 Emphasize preparation <br> action <br> recovery <br> each being important to the whole action. |

**Apparatus activities**

Specific tasks for each section: *give only one at a time*. Allow the children to have sufficient time at each section to achieve quality before moving on. Introduce task 2 the second time around.

*Specific tasks for each group*

| | |
|---|---|
| Group 1: a) Walk along bench, hurdle step to the springboard, spring off to land on mat. <br> b) Slow run along bench, hurdle step to the springboard. Immediately take off and vary shape of jump on to mat. | 1 a) Ensure children take off from correct part of springboard. A chalk mark will help. <br> b) Use very little knee bend in take off from springboard. (See *Specific Skills Guide —* Jumping.) |

| Content | Teaching points |
|---|---|

**Group 2:** a) Take two steps, jump to swing on rope to land on mat.
b) Take two steps, spring and grip high up the rope, release and land on mat facing the place you started from.

2 a) Ensure rope not 'snaking' — tension in body. Arms held bent on rope to keep body 'alive' and not just hanging. Strong leg thrust and arm release for landing.

**Group 3:** a) Begin on bench, take weight on hands and push off to floor. Roll away from landing.
b) Walk to near top of bench. Take weight on to hands on stool and push off to take feet round stool to land on mat.

3 a) Just as if on the floor — lunge step forward/reach forward — careful and controlled .
b) Grip sides of stool with hands as follow

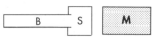

**Group 4:** a) Squat jump form floor to box — step and spring off on to mat.

4 a) hands/feet action for squat jump. Try to get as far along box as possible. Aim for continuity for the two actions. Strong push up into high jump — safe/neat landing.

b) Squat jump onto the box. Lie on the box. Place hands carefully on the mat and do a forward roll.

b) Teacher remains at this station until all children have been checked for accuracy.

**Group 5:** a) Practise swinging legs from one side of bench to the other by taking weight on hands. Develop by gaining *flight* in second phase from hands.
b) From floor, squat jump or get on to stool, lunge step into weight on hands and push to land on mat.

5 a) Hips as high as possible therefore strong thrust and swing from initial take off. (Revise 'give' in arms). Control legs into landing position.
b) Hands flat — arms prepare for receiving weight on the bench

**Group 6:** a) Revise round off.
b) From short approach run, skip step into round off and take into another springing action.

6 a) See Session 7.
b) As body is facing the original starting place the second action needs care. A step in between the two actions may be needed.

| Content | Teaching points |
|---|---|

*Note*: these tasks all have constraining limitations. Control is essential in this kind of work (which by definition has explosiveness in its execution) — clearly defined tasks will assist:
(a) the child in his efficient and safe landing of springing actions;
(b) the teacher in ensuring safety, and useful feedback.

As competence and confidence increases, so more complex (linking sections) tasks related to springing may be set. *E.g.* show a series of three different springing actions on to, across, over, off from, etc. your apparatus, OR (working between 2 SECTIONS):

'Begin on the apparatus or mats, spring off from hands, cross the floor to the second section and arrive on the apparatus from a second springing action.'

Apparatus away.
Stand well.

## Apparatus pattern

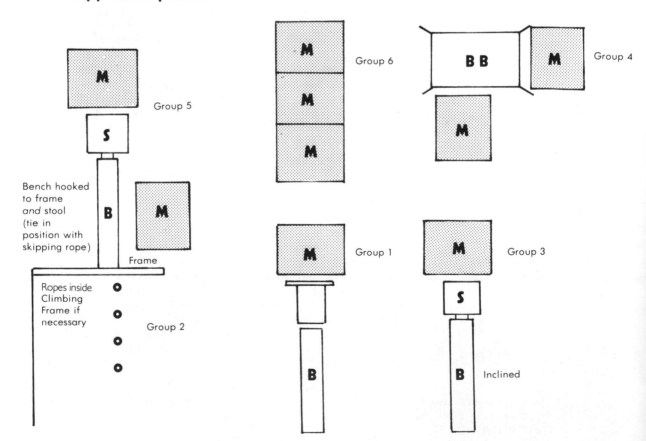

Note: Group 2 & 5 Use ropes & wall frame separately.

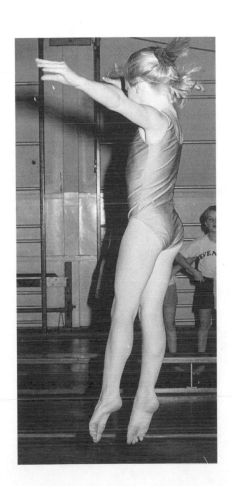

# YEAR 5

## Autumn Term:  Assessment and consolidation sessions

The children should now be able to:

1 Devise simple partner sequences based on *'following'* partners —
related to TRAVELLING.

2 Show understanding of turning actions into and out of balance —
related to ROTATION.

3 Include the cartwheel in their repertoire of basic skills and have
experience of the round off.

4 Show understanding of general principles related to springing and
landing.

More specifically:
a) demonstrate hurdle step as the stage prior to take off after the
approach run;
b) flight on to and from ropes (where possible);
c) begin to gain flight from hands.
d) perform a squat jump onto a box.

Use these sessions to revise or reinforce any of these aspects and also
any sessions which the children particularly enjoyed.

**For your notes and comments:**

# YEAR 5

**Spring Term:** TRAVELLING
**Session 1:** Bridging

| | Content | Teaching points |
|---|---|---|
| **Warm up** | 1 Running, changing direction with a turning jump. | 1 Do not anticipate the turn on take off — use arms correctly. Spring *up* from landing to aid continuity. |
| **Body preparation** | 1 On hands and knees, try to touch knee to forehead underneath the body and foot to head above body (4 times each leg) | 1 Slow stretching action. |
| | 2 Lie on back, raise legs and chest to 'V' sit, lower. | 2 Repeat × 6. |
| | 3 Practise handstands, cartwheels, round offs. | 3 Emphasize preparatory lunge step. Tension throughout body. |

## Apparatus activities

Apparatus

Climbing frame: all benches: all boxes/tables/stools: all mats. Arrange as separate items. Ensure ample spacing between apparatus. Disperse children to work at a single piece of apparatus or mat.

General tasks for *all* apparatus

| | |
|---|---|
| 1 Use your body to bridge:<br>  a) floor to apparatus (or mat)<br>  b) across apparatus<br>  c) part of apparatus to another part. | 1 An exploratory phase. Children need to have *tension* in order to hold 'bridges' with control. Look for variety of body parts in contact, for variety of body shapes created, variety of distance between contact points (need *not* be far away if height is needed). |

| Content | Teaching points |
|---|---|
| 2 Change to a different kind of apparatus and repeat 1. (Try to choose a piece of apparatus quite close to the first piece). | 2 As above. |
| 3 Now think of ways that you can travel from the bridge on your first piece of apparatus to another bridge on the second piece. | 3 Remind children of the different kinds of actions they should be trying (rolling, wheeling, springing, etc.) |
| 4 Now make this into a movement phrase where the 2 bridges *and* the travelling action are all equally important. | 4 Again give time for children to perfect this. They will need to work on the transition from the bridge into the travel. |

Apparatus away

### Final activity

Take press up position and try to clap hands before quickly returning hands to floor. Repeat several times.

Then:
Stand well.

Arm and general strengthener.

# YEAR 5

**Spring Term:** TRAVELLING
**Session 2:** Bridging

|  | Content | Teaching points |
|---|---|---|
| **Warm up** | 1 Free running, constantly changing direction. | 1 Crisp, precise changes. Clear footwork. |
| **Body preparation** | 1 Practise handstands trying to place feet in a different position on landing. | 1 Use strong trunk twist in these actions. |
|  | 2 a) Sitting — foot circling<br>b) Lying on back, legs raised, parting and closing. | 2 a) Stretch hard in all directions<br>b) Forwards and backwards, outwards and inwards. Keep legs straight. |

**Apparatus activities**

Apparatus as Session 1

| General tasks for all apparatus | |
|---|---|
| 1 Using pieces other than mats, practise:<br>a) balancing against<br>b) bridging. | 1 Feel the difference between the two. |
| 2 Now begin about 2 metres away from the apparatus. Balance, move off balance → into travel → into bridging using the apparatus. | 2 Emphasize 'perching' then *conscious* going off balance. Encourage children to repeat this several times to find variety. |

| Content | Teaching points |
|---|---|
| 3 Using a mat, floor space and a single piece of apparatus develop a phrase which uses the words BALANCE, TRAVEL, BRIDGE. It should contain at least 4 actions. | 3 Bridging and balancing are included as actions. Again emphasize the differences between the 3 action words. |

Apparatus away

**Final activity**

Lie on front — raise legs and head, hold for 5, lower. Repeat.

Then:
Stand well.

Back strengthener.

# YEAR 5

|  | Spring Term: | **PARTNER WORK** |
|---|---|---|
|  | Sessions 3 and 4: | **Copying partner using bridging, balancing and travelling** |

|  | **Content** | **Teaching points** |
|---|---|---|
| **Warm up** | 1 Running: on 'Right' touch right hand on floor, on 'Left' left hand and on 'Squat', both hands. | 1 Crisp, precise actions moving purposefully back into running. |
| **Body preparation** | 1 Straddle sit, press tummy to floor: press, press, press and relax. Repeat. | 1 Pressing not forcing. Legs straight and as wide as is confortable. Then press just a little wider. |
|  | 2 From support, walk arms round feet. | 2 Keep feet fixed. Let stronger children jump their hands round. |
|  | 3 Practise cartwheels. Then round offs. | 3 Children to be conscious of the different finishing positions of the two actions. |
| **Apparatus activities** | Apparatus as in Sessions 1 and 2 | |
|  | General task for all apparatus | |
|  | In pairs: | |
|  | 1 Using *either* a mat, *or* a single piece of apparatus find balances which match each other. | 1 Children will experiment for a considerable time on tasks 1 and 2. Still emphasize 'perching'. At this stage do not allow contact with partner. |
|  | 2 Repeat using other piece (*i.e.* not used in task 1). | |

| Content | Teaching points |
|---|---|
| | |

**Content**

3 Now using first one piece then the other find matching balances which move off balance and into a travelling action (also matching).

4 Remember ideas found in 1–3. Now similarly try out bridging actions which match those of your partner.

5 Now experiment with bridge → travel.

6 Use ideas already practised and make up a short sequence with your partner (copying) using the words BALANCE: TRAVEL: BRIDGE. Use a mat, the floor and a piece of apparatus.

**Teaching points**

3 Emphasize experimenting. Remind of actions of travelling. Children must know when off balance happens. Each part should have equal importance.

5 Transition will need care.

6 This will take time. Fairly short sequences rather than long rambling sequences will aid clarity.

**Final activity**

With your partner, following my leader squat jumping around a mat or a piece of apparatus.

Leg strengthener.

Apparatus away.
Stand well.

# YEAR 5

## Application of basic skills to new situations

These three sessions aim to develop children's ability to use basic skills in new ways. Further lessons in partner work will then ask children to include these aspects in their work.

| | Content | Teaching points |
|---|---|---|
| **Warm up** | 1 Run hurdle step jump and land. Repeat several times. | 1 Short purposeful run into accurate jumping action. |
| **Body preparation** | 1 Try to grasp right hand to left behind back (right hand over shoulder). | 1 Repeat on other side. |
| | 2 Sit, legs forward, press trunk down to legs. Press, press, press and relax. Repeat. | 2 Slow stretching action — not forced. |
| | 3 Front support, clap hands quickly replacing hands on floor. | 3 Push from floor. Try to maintain tension in trunk. |
| **Apparatus activities** | Specific tasks for each group. Seven groups select five or six of these. | |
| | Group 1: Ropes/bench. Swing on rope to land on bench. | 1 See Session 8 Autumn Term for correct use of rope. |
| | Group 2: Climbing frame. Handstand to rest balanced against the frame. | 2 Controlled lunge into inversion so that legs feel when they touch. Tension essential. Teacher remain at this station. |
| | Group 3: Bench. Cartwheel across bench — one hand on bench and one on floor on opposite side. | 3 Remind of correct placement 'lunge' foot and of hands. (See *Specific Skills Guide* — Cartwheel.) |
| | Group 4: Low nesting table. Practise handstands on top. Then twist hips to place feet at the side back to floor. | 4 Grip sides. Push from feet to raise hips with control. Deliberate placement. Complete control is essential. |

| Content | Teaching points |
|---|---|
| Group 5: Bench — box. Begin on bench, push into forward roll along box. | 5 Control legs as they finish the action to prevent over rotation to floor. Grip box tightly. |
| Group 6: Bench — springboard: mat. Begin $\frac{1}{2}$ way along bench, run, hurdle step to springboard. Show stretched, tucked, straddle, piked, wide shapes in flight from springboard. | 6 See Session 8 Autumn Term for correct hurdle action. |
| Group 7: Mats. Forward roll: come out one foot in front of the other and move straight into cartwheel. | 7 Emphasize the transition — correct placement of 'lunge' foot prior to cartwheel. |

Allow the children sufficient time to master the activities before changing.

## Final activity

Apparatus away.
Stand well.

## Apparatus pattern

# YEAR 5

**Spring Term:** **PARTNER WORK**
**Sessions 8 and 9:** **Applying basic skills to copy/matching partner**

| | Content | Teaching points |
|---|---|---|
| **Warm up** | 1 Children to devise their own free running, jumping, bouncing pattern. | 1 Good use of space. |
| **Body preparation** | 1 a) Kneeling, hands on floor, alternately round and arch back.<br>b) repeat touching forehead with knee and then back of head with foot.<br><br>2 Practise handstands, cartwheels, round offs and catsprings. | *Or*, children devise their own body preparation tasks. |

**Apparatus activities**

Apparatus Pattern as in previous sessions.

*Apparatus*

1 Climbing frame ⎱ If these constitute the same piece of equipment it
2 Ropes/bench ⎰ will not affect the tasks. Children can do different
tasks at different places on the apparatus.

3 Benches
4 Box top/low tables/bench with mat on top
5 Bench — springboard
6 Bench to box/table

In the space available set out as many of the above arrangements as possible. Allocate an arrangement to each pair of children. (*i.e.* if you have several extra benches and sufficient space then apparatus 3 and 4 could have additional couples).

| Content | Teaching points |
|---|---|

**Content**

General tasks for all apparatus

1 With your partner make a sequence copying your partner but incorporating specifically at section:

At section 1. Handstand
At section 2. Swing to land on bench
At section 3. Cartwheel across bench
At section 4. Headstand
At section 5. Run, hurdle step jump (You will have to follow partner here!)
At section 6. Forward roll along box/table

*Note*: Children will not have time to experience all sections. Do not change the children to a new section until they have produced good quality work which should now be quite skilful. Do not accept mediocrity.

Apparatus away.

**Teaching points**

Copying does not necessarily mean happening at the same time. Equally the action can be copied at a different place (*e.g.* roll along box, roll along floor).

Important to allow children time to experiment. Encourage them to play with ideas *before* making this sequence. This is essential for good sequence development. Encourage quite short sequences to aid clarity and quality.

**Final activity**

Lie flat on back. Tense body throughout — hold for 5 and relax repeat.

Then:
Stand well.

General body tension.

# YEAR 5

**PARTNER WORK**

**Matching exactly and following/copying partner**

This session encourages the children to apply past experience to a more open ended task. The apparatus should now determine the possible movement content. (*e.g.* a springboard should develop a jumping/landing emphasis to the sequence.)

| | Content | Teaching points |
|---|---|---|
| **Warm up** | 1 Move from feet to hands to feet continuously. | 1 Children should think ahead as placement of feet should lead into next movement on to hands. |
| **Body preparation** | 1 In pairs, face partners, hold wrists — sawing action with partner resisting. | 1 Maintain strong and stable foot position for this. |
| | 2 Individually sit cross legged — put head on floor between knees. | 2 Press a little further than is comfortable. |

**Apparatus activities**

Use all available apparatus arranged as single pieces. Mats may be a 'piece' or may be placed by other pieces. Allocate pairs of children to different single pieces.

General task to all pieces:

| **Content** | **Teaching points** |
|---|---|
| 1 Make up a 'longer than usual' sequence where sometimes you match your partner's actions *exactly*, and other times you follow. (Action need not necessarily be the same when following). Let the apparatus suggest the movements you can do. | 1 Danger of it 'rambling on' — encourage, after considerable experimentation, clear starting and finishing positions.<br><br>Be aware of lowering of standards. Remind the children of the movement content already experienced this term. |

Apparatus away.

**Final activity**

| | |
|---|---|
| In pairs try to turn partner over — partner resists. | General body tension. |
| | |
| Then:<br>Stand well. | |

# YEAR 5

## Spring Term: Assessment and consolidation sessions

It is unlikely that all children will have had time to experience all aspects of this term's work.

Use these sessions to extend the children's experience in elements they missed, or reinforce aspects still lacking quality.

The children should now be able to:

(a) Differentiate between matching and following in partner work.
(b) Show greater quality in the Specific Skills.
(c) Make up their own sequences.
(d) Work sensibly and co-operatively with a partner.

**For your notes and comments:**

# YEAR 6

**Autumn Term:** **ROTATION**
**Session 1:** **Twisting with turning**

| | Content | Teaching points |
|---|---|---|
| **Warm up** | 1 Run softly in and out of each other, on command jump gently in air and turn to land in a different direction. | 1 Controlled, alert as to good use of space. Deep landing from turning jump. |
| **Body preparation** | 1 On hands and knees, try to touch knee to forehead underneath the body and foot to head above body. (4 times each leg). | 1 An activity to assist back mobility — must be done with *slow* stretching, not jerkily. |
| | 2 Straddle sit, press tummy to floor. | 2 Legs as wide as possible — keep them straight throughout. |
| | 3 Practise handstands, cartwheels, round-offs. | 3 Look for good initial position, lunge, swing. TENSION through middle of body and legs. |
| **Floor activities** | 1 Quite low to the floor show different ways of travelling with a TWIST beginning each new action. | 1 Reiterate *e.g.* twist → roll twist → hands and feet actions. |
| | 2 Begin on knees — fix them firmly as the base — twist arms and shoulders round as far as they will go then CONTINUE moving in THAT DIRECTION. | 2 Importance of holding base fixed as long as possible (not swivelling) and following in the direction of the twist. Help individuals as necessary. It is likely to be a rolling action following the twist. |
| | 3 Find another base and repeat. | 3 As above. |

126

| Content | Teaching points |
|---|---|
| 4 Repeat (using different bases) but this time ensure that the resultant action is a turning action. | 4 *i.e.* using a twist to initiate a turn. Reiterate different kinds of turn. (See Year 4 — Rotation.) |
| 5 Go up into a handstand — twist hips and bring feet down in new direction → let this lead into a turning action. | 5 A demonstration will help here — legs together to finish will also help. |
| 6 From feet fixed as a base, twist to take weight on hands. (*The body changes direction* as it twists and turns). | 6 Begin in squat and gradually increase size of the action. Discuss how the twist takes the body into a turning action in the direction *of the original twist.* |
| | Contrast this to: |
| 7 Begin on feet, twist top half of body, bend knees slightly, let twist uncoil and use the recoil to take you into a turning jump. | 7 An example of how the recoil effect of a twist takes the body *away* from the direction of the twist. |
| 8 Try other bases and twist into recoil into turn. | 8 Seat, knees, shoulders. Gently at first — becoming more dynamic as children find out where the action will take them. |
| 9 Use ideas 1–8 and now make an action phrase of twists into turns; including jumping, rolling, balancing and a handstand. | 9 A complex task but it should be within the children's capabilities. If necessary break it down into smaller parts *e.g.* do first 2 actions twist — turn twist — turn What kinds of turn are they? Where can you include a handstand? Does it end 'twist into another turn' etc.? |

**Final activity**

In pairs.
A hold partner's feet, B (knees bent) bring head to knees rapidly 10 times.
Change role.

Then:
Stand well.

Stomach strengthener.

# YEAR 6

**Autumn Term:** **ROTATION**
**Sessions 2 and 3:** **Twisting with turning**

| | Content | Teaching points |
|---|---|---|
| **Warm up** | 1 Running, changing on command to side slipping. | 1 Feel difference between the two actions. Stretch legs on sideways action. |
| | 2 Travel from feet to hands to feet continually. | 2 Use twists to help the continuity here (ref. Session 1). Tension and stretching. |
| **Body preparation** | 1 Lie on back, knees bent, arch body to take weight on feet and shoulders. | 1 Keep feet firmly in place and try not to slide. |
| | 2 Stand, feet astride. Hip circling. | 2 Keep trunk from bending. |
| | 3 In pairs one squats down and tries to stand up while partner pushes down on shoulders. | 3 Repeat twice with each partner. |

**Apparatus activities**

6 groups

| General tasks for all apparatus | There will not be time for children to experience all sections. (Two or possibly 3). |
|---|---|
| 1 Crossing, moving over, under through, round, etc. the apparatus, use turning and twisting actions. | 1 A general exploratory task to give the children a feel for the section. |
| 2 Balance on, or partly on, the apparatus, twist to turn and leave the apparatus. | 2 Fix base (use hands if necessary) as before — feel full twist before moving into turn. |

| Content | Teaching points |
|---|---|
| 3 Repeat but hands must touch ground first. | 3 How can parts of the body assist in holding the base firm? |
| 4 Begin with inverted balance, twist for feet to touch ground first. | 4 Stretch high away from apparatus before twist grip with hands and reach for the ground with legs. |
| 5 Repeat 4 and take into *roll* away from apparatus. | 5 Land in control before roll. (Fluency). |
| 6 Twist, recoil and spring on to the apparatus — repeat finding other places this can happen. | 6 Begin facing a different direction — land firmly and cleanly — grip with hands if necessary. |
| 7 Begin on one part of the apparatus, twist and turn to arrive on a different part of the apparatus. | 7 Is it possible to make the movement stretch further? Tension required. |
| 8 Develop a sequence of: approach the apparatus with a turning action, twist and arrive on it; use another action to change places on the apparatus and leave with a turning action. | 8 Give time to practise this. (If too many children, they can practise elements on floor space). |

## Final activity

Apparatus away.
Stand well.

## Apparatus pattern

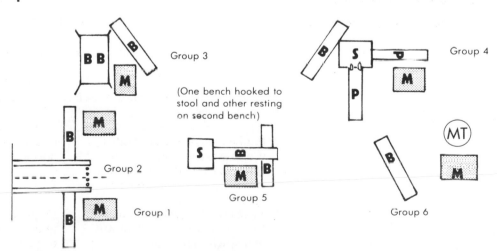

Group 3

(One bench hooked to stool and other resting on second bench)

Group 4

Group 2

Group 1

Group 5

Group 6

# YEAR 6

**Autumn Term:**    **PARTNER WORK**
**Sessions 4 and 5:**    Following and copying with twisting and turning

| | Content | Teaching points |
|---|---|---|
| **Warm up** | 1 Run, jump and land, incorporating $\frac{1}{4}$ turn into the jump. | 1 Try to precede each jump with a 'hurdle' step. Use arms correctly in turning jump (see *Specific Skills Guide —* Jumping). |
| **Body preparation** | 1 Lie on stomach, grip ankles and try to straighten legs. | 1 Move as far as possible then press a little more. |
| | 2 Kneel, hands on floor, reach under one arm with the other twisting to reach as far as possible. | 2 Repeat × 2 on each side. |
| | 3 Practise handstands, cartwheels, and round offs. | 3 Emphasize lunge step — emphasize reach with stretched arms. Good style should now be evident. |

**Apparatus activities**

Apparatus as Sessions 2 and 3

Children now working in pairs at a section they have not yet experienced.

*General taks for all apparatus* — Select from these — do not include them all in one lesson.

| | |
|---|---|
| 1 Find places on the apparatus where you can begin together (gripping apparatus), twist to leave apparatus and roll away. | 1 Encourage different starting positions. |
| 2 Start together, twist and turn to arrive *against* the apparatus and synchronize your movements. | 2 Begin far enough away for this to be possible. Which direction do you need to face to begin? |

| Content | Teaching points |
|---|---|
| **Content** | **Teaching points** |
| 3 One begin on apparatus and one on *floor* in matching balances. *Twist* and *turn* from the balance to exchange places. Find other ways of doing this same task. | 3 The actions in between the balances need not necessarily match. Start at different places. Use different balances. Use different travelling actions. |
| 4 Follow and copy partner using your apparatus. Include a handstand with twist to land, somewhere in the phrase. | 4 Keep 'phrase' short. Insist that the work is skilful and incorporates work already practised. |
| 5 Make up a short sequence which 'matches' exactly at times and 'follows' at times using twists to take you into turns. | 5 In matching aim for synchronization of timing — less important in the 'following' element. If the work becomes 'meandering' remind children of the repertoire of skills they should be including in their work. |

**Final activity**

Apparatus away.
Stand well.

# YEAR 6

**Autumn Term:** **PARTNER WORK**
**Session 6:** **Obstacles: related to turning into and out of balance**

Obstacles can be still or moving. Partners can negotiate with and without contact.

Least complex therefore is still obstacles ⎱
                               no contact ⎰

The work builds from this to moving obstacles and no contact, to still obstacles with contact.

|  | Content | Teaching points |
|---|---|---|
| **Warm up** | 1 Running, interchanging with bouncing on spot (on command). | 1 Instant change. Feel difference between two types of action. |
|  | 2 Travel feet to hands to feet by twisting and turning. | 2 Use the twists to change direction stretch and feel the tension when inverted. |
| **Body preparation** | 1 Sitting: foot circling. | 1 Stretch hard in all directions. |
|  | 2 Standing: ankle springing, leading to bouncing. | 2 Do not move to bouncing too quickly. |
| **Floor activities** | 1 Individually. Quickly remind yourself of different methods of travelling and turning. | 1 Articulate: parts to turn on, kinds of turn. Extension in legs important. |
|  | 2 From stillness, twist into a turning action and hold a balance. Find several variations of this. | 2 Hold base, twist as far as possible — turn must travel — clear balance at end. (These two tasks are by way of revision prior to partner tasks). |

| Content | Teaching points |
|---|---|
| 3 In 2s. A holds a balance and B finds turning actions to go over, under, round, through etc. Then reverse roles. | 3 Free practice of a range of ideas. Articulate the good ideas children are showing. NO CONTACT. |
| 4 A holds tucked balance. B practises turning jumps to negotiate. Reverse roles. | 4 Remind of preparation for the jump. Clear landing. |
| 5 B holds tucked balance. A practises feet → hands → feet turning actions to negotiate. Then reverse roles. | 5 Long reach over obstacle as in preparation for cartwheel — lunge position essential. Control and care important. |
| 6 In turn, find balances with space between body and floor which partner can do rolling turns under or through. | 6 Need to stretch high and away from the floor. Care with legs as obstacle is negotiated — they may need to be tucked into body. |
| 7 Develop a pattern of two actions thus:<br>A obstacle B turns to negotiate<br>B obstacle A turns to negotiate<br>As B finishes first action he becomes the obstacle. A tries to make the movement from his first balance part of the preparation for the turning action over B. | 7 Again children must explore a range of possibilities first, before moulding them into the pattern. Continuity is the most difficult to achieve — it merits some time being given to it. |

**Final activity**

| In pairs A tries to turn B over, B resists. Change role. | General body tension. |
|---|---|

Then:
Stand well.

# YEAR 6

**Autumn Term:** **PARTNER WORK**
**Session 7:** **Moving obstacles: related to travelling**

|  | Content | Teaching points |
|---|---|---|
| **Warm up** | 1 Run down one side of hall and side slip across other side — repeat. | 1 All children moving in the same direction. Push hard on side slipping. |
|  | 2 Practise run, jump and land. | 2 Spring *up* from landing fully before running on. |
| **Body preparation** | 1 Squat thrusts × 10. | 1 No more at this stage of the session. |
|  | 2 Practise handstands, cartwheels round offs and catsprings. | 2 Good tension. Use lunge step effectively where appropriate. |
| **Floor activities** | 1 In 2s remind yourselves of the different ways of moving over, under, round a partner. | 1 See Session 6. |
|  | 2 Now try out some activities where the obstacle SLOWLY moves in a clear action across the floor. | 2 No contact. Articulate the various ideas children find. Keep changing roles. |
|  | 3 One partner tries a slow stretched rolling obstacle — what different ways can this be negotiated by the other partner? Try it moving away from and towards partner. | 3 In turn try jumping, and hands/feet actions. |

| **Content** | **Teaching points** |
|---|---|
| 4 Repeat with tucked rolling obstacle. | 4 As above. |
| 5 Develop a sequence of 4 actions: A obstacle, B negotiates, B obstacle, A negotiates (repeated) — where the obstacle is moving twice and in balance (still) twice. | 5 This will need time — especially if fluency is to be developed. Encourage simplicity, clarity, quality. |

**Final activity**

| | |
|---|---|
| Lie on front: raise legs and head (and as much of chest as possible) off floor. Hold for 6. Lower. Repeat. | Back strengthener. |

Then:
Stand well.

# YEAR 6

**Autumn Term:** **PARTNER WORK**
**Session 8:** **Contact with obstacles: related to Balance**

| | Content | Teaching points |
|---|---|---|
| **Warm up** | 1 Running and jumping showing clear and different body shapes during flight. | 1 Run should purposefully lead into hurdle step into jump. Spring up from landing to aid continuity. |
| **Body preparation** | 1 a) Happy cat/angry cat<br>b) arm circling backwards — sitting back on heels in kneeling position.<br>c) All fours — move slowly forwards and backwards over arms. | 1 Stretch body into all the positions with easy pressure — not forcing actions. |
| | 2 Take weight on hands and push to come back to feet. | 2 'Give' a little and thrust strongly from arms. |

**Mat to floor activities**

Children will have to alternate between working on mats and working on the floor. Use all the mats.

| | | |
|---|---|---|
| | 1 In 2s experiment now with the obstacle being a SUPPORT for the other to balance against. | 1 ONLY if the children are controlled and strong enough. Importance of strong firm base. Explain this clearly to the children. Remind of different balances — can one part of body be *on* partner instead of floor? Take time over this section. This requires a lot of teacher control. |

| **Content** | **Teaching points** |
|---|---|
| 2  With care find an action which will take you towards your partner (the obstacle) and into the balance (as in 1). Change roles. | 2  *e.g.* Rolling into the balance jumping into the balance wheeling into the balance Again give time. |
| 3  Put together the following: A = strong obstacle B = moves into balance against A, holds balance then moves away and becomes a strong obstacle. A then moves towards B and holds a balance against B. | 3  The movements into and out of the balances must be as important as the balances. Encourage full experimentation before perfection. |

**Final activity**

| | |
|---|---|
| Squat jumping round mat trying to catch the person in front. | Body must remain in squat position throughout. Leg strengthener. |

Then:
Stand well.

# YEAR 6

**Autumn Term: Sessions 9 and 10:**

## FURTHER DEVELOPMENT OF BASIC SKILLS

In these lessons the basic skills are applied to new situations. Some children may still need to practise earlier stages. They should be encouraged to do the activities suggested in brackets.

| Content | Teaching points |
|---|---|
| **Warm up** | | |

**Warm up**

Content
1 Children devise their own warm up.

Teaching points
1 If the children still seem inexperienced use ideas from earlier sessions.

**Body preparation**

1 Children devise their own body preparation

**Group work**

8 groups (select 5 or 6 to suit your situation and arrange accordingly).

1 Bench inclined to low rung of stool: mat (note placement).: + extra mat

2 Benches

3 Ropes: bench

4 Plank inclined to low rung of climbing frame (if same apparatus as ropes it may still be used as a separate group). Mat on plank.

5 Springboard: mat

6 Bench: Bar box: mat (+ separate mat)

7 Movement Table: mats

8 Length of mats.

| Content | Teaching points |
|---|---|
| *Specific tasks to different groups* | |
| Group 1: Backward roll down bench covered by mat finishing feet astride bench. Take weight on one foot and move straight into cartwheel. (Or, practise backward roll across mat into standing, twist to cartwheel). | 1 Grip bench — work hard on hands to clear head of bench. Stretch legs to reach floor. Work on good transition. Start *low down* bench. |
| Group 2: Begin on bench: cartwheel off end of bench placing first hand on bench and second on floor. (Or, practise cartwheels across bench putting first hand on bench and second on floor.) | 2 Controlled lowering lunge step needed. Drop in height will accelerate the end of the action. |
| Group 3: Swing from rope to land on bench facing ropes. Let go. As rope returns jump on to it and swing back to starting place. (Or, practise swinging from rope to land on bench.) | 3 Need to turn before landing. Ensure rope is not snaking before jumping on to it. |
| Group 4: From floor forward roll *up* the incline. Finish in straddle either side of plank. Push off to one foot and move into a round off. (Or, practise round offs on floor.) | 4 Gentle push needed to raise hips and help the rotation up the plank. Stretch legs after push. Use hands correctly to help you to stand in a straddle. (See *Specific Skills Guide* — Rolling.) |
| Group 5: 5 stride approach run, hurdle step from floor to springboard. Jump to land on mat. | 5 This happened naturally in earlier stage from a bench. Think of one footed take off from floor into two footed take off from springboard. |
| Group 6: Begin on bench. Push to headstand on bar box. Twist feet to land on mat. (Or, practise headstands on the separate mat). | 6 Push to initiate the inversion, then control legs into headstand. Work hard on arms — grip box. |
| Group 7: Match a movement on the Movement Table and a movement on the floor. | 7 Variety can be found by experimenting with leg shape. |

| Content | Teaching points |
|---|---|
| Group 8: Practise any combinations of skills you like which you have learned. | 8 Watch for children simply repeating the same thing. Encourage them to try other combinations. 'Do you need to begin facing the mat?' Effect of this, etc. |

Children should be encouraged to observe each other whilst waiting for their turn. The teacher may question children about the work in this respect. (*e.g.* did you see what she had to do in order to move into the round off?)

Give the children sufficient time to master these tasks and achieve quality.

If time allows, encourage the children to incorporate the required action into an action phrase.

## Final Activity

Apparatus away.
Stand well.

# YEAR 6

## Autumn Term: Assessment and consolidation sessions

The children will now have experienced:

1 Contact and non-contact partner work in different forms (refer back if necessary to Year 5) related to different movement units.

2 Further development of ROTATION (twisting and turning).

3 The application of basic skills to new situations.

4 They should be competent in:

a) The range of basic skills.

b) Developing short sequences in response to a set task.

c) Co-operating with a partner in making sequences.

d) Demonstrating good movement.

e) Appreciating others' work and commenting sensitively upon it.

Use these sessions to revise or reinforce any of these aspects (if necessary, select work from previous years), or repeat elements which were particularly enjoyed.

**For your notes and comments:**

# YEAR 6

| | Content | Teaching points |
|---|---|---|
| **Warm up** | 1 Running, alternating with bouncing on spot and side slipping. | 1 Initially call out changes, then encourage children to change in their own good time. Precise footwork — tension and stretching. |
| **Body preparation** | 1 Straddle sit — rock on to back and press thighs wider. | 1 Stretch legs — gentle pressure. |
| | 2 Lie on stomach, grip ankles, try to straighten legs. | 2 Feel stretching in the trunk. |
| | 3 Practise handstands, cartwheels and round offs. | 3 Emphasize tension at the start, reach during lunge and maintain tension. |
| **Floor activities** | 1 Develop an action phrase of spring, twist and balance. | 1 Encourage springing from hands. Twist should initiate a change of direction. Give children time to experiment with various possibilities. |
| | 2 Practise jumping and springing (feet to feet) (on to and from hands) where the body is symmetrical. | 2 Discuss notion of symmetry. |
| | 3 Practise feet — hands — feet symmetrically. | 3 Expect two footed take off on to hands and pushing *back* to feet — also catsprings. |
| | 4 Now move feet-hand-feet asymmetrically. | 4 The action may twist or lean. One hand/one foot may be used. |

| Content | Teaching points |
|---|---|
| 5 Show a symmetrical feet/hands/feet action into an asymmetrical one. | 5 Two clear actions. Think about the transition from one to another. |
| 6 Quickly try out different balances where the body is symmetrical or asymmetrical. | 6 Ask the children which they are showing. Identify which bases can only be used for symmetrically held balances. (2 feet: heads 2 hands: shoulders, etc.) |
| 7 Move into a symmetrical balance, go off balance and move into an asymmetrical balance. Try several ideas. | 7 Ensure that movements into and out of balance are controlled, purposeful and varied. |
| 8 Using ideas already practised develop a sequence to include 2 feet/hands/feet actions and 2 balances. Show symmetry and asymmetry. | 8 This picks up tasks 5 and 7 and combines them. The sequence does not have to follow the order stated in the task. |

**Final activity**

Take press up position. Clap hands, quickly returning hands to floor. Try this several times.

Then:
Stand well.

Arm and stomach strengthener.

# YEAR 6

**ACTION PHRASES: (Related to several units)**
**Emphasizing symmetry and asymmetry**

|  | **Content** | **Teaching points** |
|---|---|---|
| **Warm up** | 1 Children devise their own warm up activity. | 1 One child may lead this. |
| **Body preparation** | 1 Circle both arms in front of body<br>a) both in same direction<br>b) in opposite directions inwards<br>c) in opposite directions outwards. | 1 Ensure full range of movement. |
|  | 2 Lie on back, clasp hands and try to take legs through arms to touch floor behind head. | 2 Allow the less mobile to do this without clasping hands. |
|  | 3 Practise moving from feet to hands to feet. | 3 Push from arms strongly. |

**Apparatus activities**

All benches/box tops/low nesting tables etc. with mats spaced evenly around the hall.

*General tasks for all apparatus*

| | |
|---|---|
| 1 Find ways of bridging from floor to bench (or mat to bench/or mat to floor)<br>a) with symmetrical body line<br>b) with asymmetrical body line. | 1 Check that children fully understand differences. |

| Content | Teaching points |
|---|---|
| 2 Pick out several ideas shown and all practice. | 2 Teacher select — identify what is important about selection — (*e.g.* hands and head on mat — 1 foot on bench — is it symmetrical or asymmetrical?) |
| 3 Experiment with crossing bench<br>a) symmetrically<br>b) asymmetrically | 3 Expect skilful interpretation and good quality. |
| 4 a) some try ways of moving along bench as above.<br>b) others use mat to practise moving symmetrically, then asymmetrically: then asymmetrically into asymmetrical balance (and vice versa). | 4 a) if necessary children can touch floor as they move along<br>b) encourage children to twist and be quite free in second part of task.<br>Show a variety of ideas to class. |
| 5 Develop an action phrase based on bridging, balancing and travelling — showing symmetry and asymmetry. | 5 Children to select from ideas already practised. |

**Final activity**

| | |
|---|---|
| Feet under bench (knees bent) bring head to knees rapidly 10 times. | Stomach strengthener. |

Apparatus away.
Stand well.

# YEAR 6

**PARTNER WORK**
**Sharing space emphasizing symmetry and asymmetry**

|  | Content | Teaching points |
|---|---|---|
| **Warm up** | 1 In 2s A travel around hall changing from running to jumping and landing and to side slipping: B follows. Change role. | 1 It must be purposeful and clear. Spring up from landing to aid continuity. |
|  | 2 Individually. Practise moving from feet to hands to feet. | 2 Continuous action — use twist. Tension and stretching in whole body. |
| **Body preparation** | 1 Caterpillar walk. | 1 Fix hands and gradually walk feet towards them (legs straight). |
|  | 2 Kneeling, hands on floor, reach under one arm with the other twisting to reach as far as possible. | 2 Use twist fully. |
|  | 3 Take weight on hands and place feet in different place on landing. | 3 Again twist fully to make this possible. |

|  | **Content** | **Teaching points** |
|---|---|---|

**Apparatus activities**

Use all available (and appropriate) apparatus as single pieces in their own space. Mats separate from apparatus. Large pieces (*e.g.* frames) can be used by several couples.

Allocate pairs of children to a piece where the space on which they work is defined clearly. (This will only take a minute or two).

*General tasks for all apparatus: working in pairs.*

1 Experiment with ways in which you both are moving in the confined space of floor or apparatus. (Not copying or following necessarily). Go over, under, round partner sometimes. Vary the actions you use.

1 Take time over this phase. Show one or two ideas to the class to stimulate variety. Remind of bridging, balancing, twisting, travelling, springing. There may be times when one is momentarily still whilst other negotiates.

2 Now together make up a short sequence based on some of your ideas in 1 but emphasizing symmetry and asymmetry.

2 There may well be copying, following negotiating partner. Also may balance/bridge against partner at times.

**Final activity**

Apparatus away.
Stand well.

# YEAR 6

| | Content | Teaching points |
|---|---|---|
| **Warm up** | 1 Running, changing direction with a turning jump. Repeat. | 1 Precede jump with a hurdle step. Use arms correctly during the turn. |
| **Body preparation** | 1 On all fours, touch knees to forehead, then foot to back of head. Change legs. Repeat several times. | 1 A slow pressure not a forced action. |
| | 2 Remain on all fours. Gently move body forwards over arms and then backwards. | 2 Keep hands flat. Again slow pressure. |
| | 3 Practise handstands, cartwheels and round offs. | 3 These actions should now be of good quality and together should clearly show their differences. |
| **Floor activities** | 1 Develop a phrase of *actions* which illustrate the words tuck, stretch and twist. | 1 A task demanding that the children recall experience from travelling, balancing, rotation and springing units. Encourage experimentation. |
| | 2 Try different *actions* where the body is generally tucked. | 2 Expect weight on hands with legs tucked, tucked jumps, rolls, balances, etc. |
| | 3 Repeat with stretched actions. | 3 Bending/curling may be necessary to initiate some actions. |
| | 4 Repeat with actions that include a twist. | 4 Twist into action, twist during action, twist out of action. |

| Content | Teaching points |
|---|---|
| **Content** | **Teaching points** |
| 5 Now experiment with changing your action *and* changing the shape *and* changing the speed. | 5 *E.g.* quick tucked jump into slow stretched balance. Stay with this for a while in order to find many possibilities. |
| 6 Now revise and modify your original phrase (Task 1), to show change of speed and change of shape. | 6 Encourage children to use ideas practised in Tasks 2–5 to make their work more challenging. |

**Final activity**    Squat jumping leg strengthener.        A child may lead this.

Then:
Stand well.

# YEAR 6

**Spring Term:**   **PARTNER WORK**
**Session 6:**   **Contrasting speed and shape**

|  | Content | Teaching points |
|---|---|---|
| **Warm up** | 1 Run gently amongst each other on command change to sudden short burst of speed and then continue gentle running. | 1 Be alert to space you will suddenly move into. |
| **Body preparation** | 1 Lie on back, raise hips and legs, part and close legs forwards and backwards, outwards and inwards. | 1 Hold tension in legs throughout. |
|  | 2 Straddle sit, press tummy to floor. | 2 Press legs a little wider if possible. |
|  | 3 Stand. Ankle springing leading into bouncing. | 3 Strong ankle action. |

**Apparatus activities**

All mats, benches/box tops separately spaced. In pairs, children choose to work on bench or mat.

*General tasks to all pieces*

| Content | Teaching points |
|---|---|
| 1 Together, using your apparatus find actions which you both can do quickly. (You need not copy exactly). | 1 Jumps, some rolls, runs, some inversions, recoil from twist, pivot etc. Encourage on to, off, across, etc. apparatus. |
| 2 Repeat looking for slow actions. | 2 Balances, bridges, preparation into twist, rolls, etc. |
| 3 Practise working together on actions where you *contrast* the speed. | 3 Remember you can cross each other, use each other, work towards, away from, etc. Show a few ideas to class. |

152

| Content | Teaching points |
|---|---|
| 4 Try now to modify some of these by *also* contrasting the shape. | 4 Remember ideas practised in earlier lessons. |
| 5 Now plan an action phrase where you *contrast* the work of your partner (by speed and shape) for the first part and then match your partner (in speed and shape) for the second part. | 5 This will take time — it will need to be a 'longer than usual' phrase so that it is not merely one contrasted action and one matching one. |

## Final activity

Apparatus away.
Stand well.

# YEAR 6

**Spring Term:**    **LINKING SPECIFIC ACTIONS**
**Sessions 7 and 8:**    **Contrasting level**

|  | **Content** | **Teaching points** |
|---|---|---|
| **Warm up** | 1 Children devise their own warm up activity. | 1 A child may lead this. |
| **Body preparation** | 1 a) Lie on back, raise each leg alternately<br>b) Sit cross-legged and put head on floor between knees. | 1 Emphasize precision of direction change — mobility in spine.<br>a) do this slowly keeping legs straight<br>b) press slowly a little further each time. |
|  | 2 Practise various methods of inverting on to hands. Travel if appropriate. | 2 Those children who are able could try to walk on hands. Tension throughout body essential. |
|  | 3 Repeat, now pushing off from hands back to feet. | 3 Use strong thrust from arms — prepare legs ready for the landing. |

**Apparatus activities**                                6 groups

Group 1. Movement Table: bench: mat

Group 2. $\frac{1}{2}$ climbing frame: ropes: bench

Group 3. Other $\frac{1}{2}$ climbing frame: 2 inclined planks (1 to be 1 metre higher than the other) 1 mat

Group 4. Stool: 1 bench inclined to top rung
                    1 bench: 1 mat

| Content | Teaching points |
|---|---|

Group 5. 2 stools/tables: 2 benches (or 1 plank and 1 bench) 1 mat (1 bench hooked between stools and bench hooked as indicated)

Group 6. Springboard: Bar box: 2 mats

*General tasks for all apparatus*

1 Find balances where you are
   a) High on your apparatus
   b) Low *on* your apparatus
   c) Inverted with feet high and hands low.

1 a) Try to make balance stretch high also
   b) Can the balances give the impression of being close to but not touching the floor, yet still feeling 'perched'.
   c) You may use floor and apparatus together.

   Give all 3 tasks so children can freely experiment.

2 Experiment with smoothly flowing actions that
   a) take you from low to high
   b) take from high to low
   c) rebound low/high/low or high/low/high.

2 Look for short series of actions which spring and twist. Suggest hands touching down first sometimes when moving from high to low. Emphasize continuity. Select and show one or two examples to help clarify the point.

3 Practise handstands where one hand is on the floor and the other gripping or pressing on a low part of the apparatus.
   or
   Practise handstands where you rest/lean on part of the apparatus.

3 Some children should practise handstands on the floor if necessary (and change over after a few turns). Begin gently to feel how the body weight distribution changes. Work hard on arms to adjust body weight. Then try to stretch feet high — tension essential.

Give the children the time to try tasks 1–3 on different apparatus arrangements before moving on to task 4.

| Content | Teaching points |
|---|---|

4  Make a sequence (individual)
which must include
a handstand
another balance
a springing action
(and other actions you
choose).
It must show changes of level
on the floor and apparatus.

4  Encourage children to
experiment freely for quite a
while in order to fully exploit
the task. Ask at times to see
the 3 specific actions in
isolation in order to ensure
their inclusion. Look at one or
two and suggest modifications/
clarifications.

Then

In pairs:

Work with your partner on
task 4 to produce any kind of
partner sequence you like.

Allow children to change their
apparatus section if necessary.
Again reiterate that 'matching'
is not necessarily required.

**Final activity**  Try to squat jump on to a low
piece of apparatus.

Remain in squat. (Put inclined
benches to floor first).
Leg strengthener.

Apparatus away.
Stand well.

# Apparatus pattern

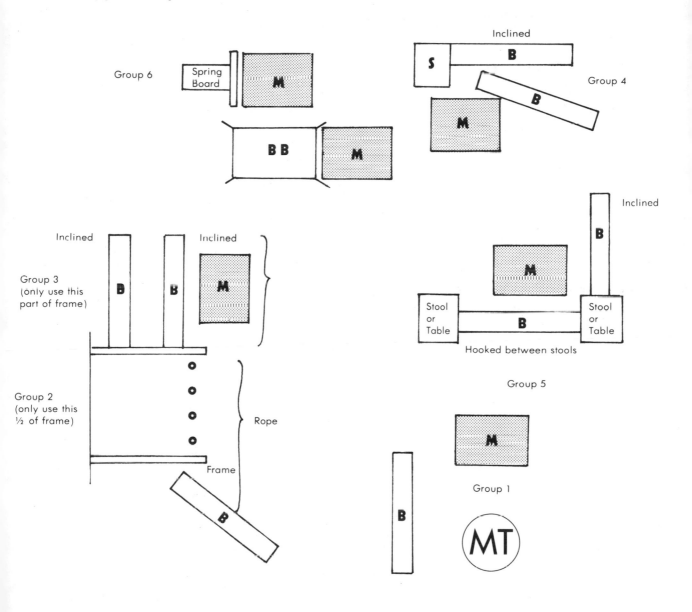

Group 6

Spring Board

M

Inclined

S

B

Group 4

B

M

B B

M

Group 3
(only use this
part of frame)

Inclined

B

Inclined

B

M

Inclined

B

M

Stool or Table

Stool or Table

B

Hooked between stools

Group 5

Group 2
(only use this
½ of frame)

Rope

Frame

B

M

Group 1

B

MT

# YEAR 6

**Spring Term:**
**Sessions 9 and 10:**

These sessions ask the children to select their own action phrase, — and apply one of six variations to the phrase (given by the teacher).

The children may choose to work alone or with a partner.

(*Note*: this open-ended approach will only be possible if the children have had a full experience of a) action phrases b) ways of using different emphases.)

| | **Content** | **Teaching points** |
|---|---|---|
| **Warm up and body preparation** | Children to select their own activity ensuring:<br>1) a running/leg activity<br>2) a mobility/strengthening activity<br>3) weight on hands practice | Coach as appropriate. |
| **Floor activities** | 1 Select an action phrase of 3 different action words. | 1 *E.g.* spring, twist and invert (Discuss/articulate *if necessary*, the possible range). |
| | 2 Select one of the following to emphasize in the phrase (and therefore develop it):<br>a) leg shape<br>b) whole body shape<br>c) symmetry/asymmetry<br>d) levels<br>e) speed<br>f) pathways | 2 a) Combinations of apart/together bent/straight<br>b) Tucked, stretched, spread, piked, straddle, twisted, arched<br>c) Emphasizing side of body stress<br>d) Relate to parts of body high — and high/low on apparatus (if selected).<br>e) Note the actions which have an inbuilt speed<br>f) This must not ramble on.<br><br>Try to encourage wide selection of a–f. |

|                    | Content | Teaching points |
|--------------------|---------|-----------------|
| **Final activity** | Apparatus away (if selected). Stand well. | |

# YEAR 6

## Spring Term: Assessment and consolidation sessions

This term has seen the development of previous work.

Sessions 9 and 10 will provide a good indication of the children's ability to both perform and show understanding of the work covered in the units.

The notes in TEACHING METHOD on page 3 in the introduction can be used as a checklist for the children's progress.

**For your notes and comments:**

# SPECIFIC SKILLS GUIDE

There are seven specific skills to be taught as follows:

1 Running
2 Jumping (including hurdle step)
3 Forward Roll
4 Backward Roll
5 Headstand
6 Handstand
7 Cartwheel
8 Round Off

**1 Running**    Running is an activity that is seldom taught and which is used mainly for warm-up purposes. Few children, as a result, run well *i.e.* in a mechanically efficient manner. Some of the faults that one can observe in children's running are pointed out below with appropriate corrective action. The teacher should use the corrective action as positive teaching points and encourage children to work on these aspects.

| *Fault* | *Correct Action* |
| --- | --- |
| Running with flat feet, producing a slapping action on the floor. | Run on the 'balls' of the feet (check child hasn't dropped arches). Encourage ankle extension. |
| Running with the feet or knees turned outwards or inwards. | Run concentrating on feet pointing ahead. Run along a line. |
| Running with straight legs. | Bend at knees and emphasize knee lift. |

Running with straight arms. (This can cause excessive twisting of the trunk from side to side).

Bend arms to 90 degrees at elbows and punch with arms. Illustrate the effect of the arms by asking children to jog on the spot and then speed up arms only. In 99 cases out of a 100, the legs will automatically increase in speed.

Running in too upright a position.

Demonstrate that little ground is covered in this way. A lean forward is necessary to produce a longer stride. This should be demonstrated to the children.

Not running in a straight line and/or head turning from side to side.

Run along a line on the floor and fix eyes on a spot ahead.

Any child who appears to have a serious problem of flat feet should be referred to his doctor for remedial treatment.

### 2 Jumping/Landing

The most important aspect of jumping, paradoxically, is landing. The children should be taught to land on the balls of the feet with immediate lowering of the heels and *slight* bend of the knees to end up in a stable position (*Fig. 1, a.b.c.*).
(Saying 'toe-heel' helps this feeling.)

*Fig. 1*

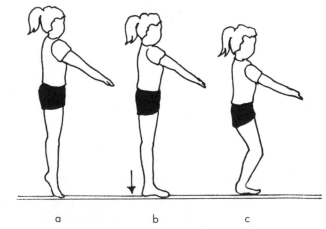

a        b        c

This should be done initially on mats to avoid jarring. The bottom should be above the heels and the back relatively straight (*1(c)*). The children should be asked to squat low and observe what happens to their heels. (The heels lift up, thus creating a small base of support and, therefore, a less stable landing position). Jumping practices should be on the spot at first, then with a couple of steps and finally after a short run. Children should try to get their feet slightly ahead of their bodies to establish a secure landing, otherwise forward momentum will cause them to over-balance forward. Later, jumps from a low height can be introduced.

**Take-off and Airbourne Phase (including Hurdle Step)**
Normally, take off is from two feet and children can experience difficulty in coordinating the step before this moment of take-off (the hurdle step).

The take off can be performed from the floor or from a springboard (or reuther board).

A useful preliminary stage is as follows: —

The child walks from half way along the bench, drops naturally onto 2 feet on the spring board and jumps up and onto the mat. (Thus the 1 foot to 2 feet pattern is established)

Develop this by a *gentle* run, rather than a walk.

Then:  the full and correct hurdle step (take off) action is as follows:

*Fig. 2(a)*
Arms back
Long, *low* jump from 1 foot
Arms begin to swing forward strongly.

*(b)*
Arms come through on approach to spring board (or take off point)

*(c)*
Arms still lifting

*(d)*
Arms assist full stretch
Legs and ankles fully extended

(Note position of arms in relation
to head)

c

d

### Jumps with quarter and half and full turns

All turning and twisting movements of this nature start whilst the feet
are in contact with the ground. The important point for the children
to understand is that as the arms lift up in the jump, the head and
shoulders turn slightly in the intended direction without any dropping
of the shoulders (*Fig. 3*). The arms must remain fairly close together if
the turn is to occur easily. To stop rotation the arms drop from above
the head to shoulder height. Body tension should be retained
throughout. A lack of tension, especially in the stomach region will
tend to cause unstable landing positions.

*Fig. 3*

**3 Forward Roll**   This should be done on mats and not on the floor.

A good general principle when teaching gymnastics skills is to start with the last part and work back to the beginning. This is not always possible but by using this method the pupil can always finish a movement and is not moving into the 'unknown' which causes stress and fear.

The finished roll should look like the drawings in *Fig. 4(a.b.c.d.e.)*.

It is important that:

    (i)    hands are flat;
    (ii)   the action goes *forward*;
    (iii)  from (*b*) a good push will ensure straight legs into the piked position as in (*c*);
    (iv)  feet then tuck in really close to the seat;
    (v)   arms reach forward and up to stand.

The teaching stages are: —

(a)  Rock backwards and forwards (*Fig. 5a, b, c.*) emphasizing heels close to bottom and chin to the chest. If the feet are away from the bottom at point (*d*) in *Fig. 4* they exert a force backwards which prevents the child standing up.
(b)  The arms should reach forward in *Fig. 5(c)* partner's hands can be caught or grasped to encourage this action.
(c)  The child stands feet astride, hands on floor near feet but shoulder width apart. He then tucks his chin to his chest and lowers top of the shoulders to the floor and tips over to roll. The moment the rolls starts he carries out the actions shown in *Fig. 4, c, d* and *e*.

*Fig. 4*

*Fig. 5*

(d)  The child attempts the roll from a squat position (*Fig. 4, b, c, d*).

**Variation of Roll Involving Shape — Forward roll to straddle stand**
This roll involves flexibility in the hips — the wider the legs the easier the move.

*Fig. 6*

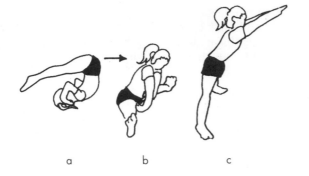

a   b   c

As the roll comes toward the ground, the legs part. Before the legs come to the ground (b) the hands reach to the ground between the legs — shoulders well in front of hips and then the hands push to bring the body up on the feet.

*Fig. 7*

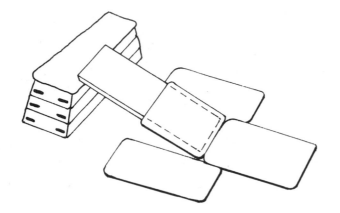

This is the best taught using the sloping plank. Mats need to be placed on the planks alongside and at the bottom of the plank (*Fig. 7*). The pupil's feet are placed either side of the planks when finishing the roll which makes the whole move much easier and above all successful. *See Fig. 8(a) (b)*

Slowly lower the planks and eventually dispense with them altogether.

*Fig. 8*

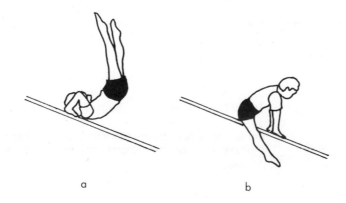

a                    b

**4 Backward Roll**   The backward roll should look like the drawings in *Fig. 9(a, b, c, d, e)*.

*Fig. 9*

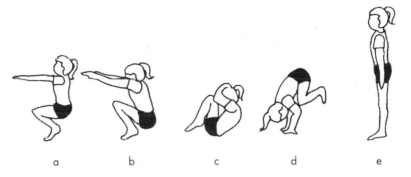

a      b      c      d      e

It is important that:

   (i)   hands are held in position early;
  (ii)   hands are placed flat on floor close to the head (fingers pointing towards feet thumbs to head);
 (iii)   knees and head are tucked tightly to chest;
 (iv)   when hips move over head push hard from the hands and stay tucked;
  (v)   keep pushing and land on *feet* (not knees).

The teaching stages are as follows:

(a) Rock backwards and forwards emphasizing heels close to the bottom and chin to the chest.

Ask children what would get in     Answer: The Head.
the way to stop them going
right over backwards?

How can the head be got out     By lifting the body over it by
of the way?     using the arms *Fig. 8(d)*.

(b) Now rock backwards and ensure that the push comes when the knees and hips are above the hands so that it lifts and does not thrust the child back from where he has come.
(c) Finally, the whole roll can be done from squat and stand (*Fig. 9 a, b, c, d, e*).
(d) A variation of the backward roll is to a straddle stand.

**5 Headstand**   The basis of a good headstand is a good base of support.

*Fig. 10*      Head

Plan view of the base of support (*Fig. 10*).

Hand      Hand

The teaching stages are:

(a) Place hands and head on mat as shown (below *Figure 11(a)*) but in kneeling position. Straighten legs (*Fig. 11(b)*) so that weight is on hands and head. Then walk carefully towards nose until bottom is over head (*Fig. 11(c)*).

*Fig. 11*

(b) Now bend legs up so that the feet are by the bottom (*Fig. 11(d)*).
(c) When this can be achieved confidently the legs can be straightened (*Fig. 11(e)*).

*Fig. 11(e)*

In order to roll out of the headstand tell the children to put 'chin to chest' and gently roll out.

**6 The Handstand**    The handstand requires strong arms and shoulder girdle and the ability of the child to hold its body tense. Without this basic body tension 'banana' type handstands with their attendant undesirable physical effects will occur. (The handstand is an inverted standing position. A plumb line dropped from the ankles should pass through the knee, hip, shoulder, wrist (*Fig. 12a*).

Correct                    Incorrect

*Fig. 12*

a                    b        c

### Teaching
Preparatory stage
1 The child should lie down on his back, arms above his head. He tenses his body. This is the feeling to be achieved when on the hands, and also the body shape required, *i.e.* a straight line.

2 He now kneels on the floor, hands flat pointing forward in front of knees. He straightens his legs (*Fig. 13(a) (b)*).

*Fig. 13*

a                    b

SAFETY
Emphasize, flat hands, fingers pointing forward, shoulder width apart. Head looking just in front of fingers.
3 Repeat 2. When legs are straight swing one up into the air straight pushing gently with the other leg and feeling the tendency for it to lift off the ground.
4 Ditto but this time exchange legs in the air — *i.e.* as first leg starts to come back to ground the second legs swings up.
5 Children stand arms above head and step forward as for handstand, and swing one leg up into the air straight, with sufficient speed to lift the other leg *just off* the ground.
6 Handstand with teacher support (*Figs. 14 and 15*)

171

*Fig. 14*
Initial support position

*Fig. 15*
Support when child is able to
perform a handstand

NB. Supporter's head by child's
hip to avoid being kicked in the
face.

7  The finished action should look like drawings in *Fig. 16*.

*Fig. 16*

It is important that:
  (i)   hands are flat, shoulder width apart; fingers forward, arms
        straight;
  (ii)  eyes look at the hands;
  (iii) the movement is 'step forward — reach forward' — gently.
        (The step forward action is the *lunge step*);
  (iv)  hips are above the shoulders and the body is straight.

SAFETY
In case of *overbalancing* — step one of the hands forward. The feet
will then come down sideways.

**7 Cartwheel**   The cartwheel as the name implies, is a wheeling action involving rotation on the 4 points of the body, hand, hand, foot, foot, each contacting the ground succesively in an even rhythm.

The finished action should look like the drawings in *Fig. 17*.

*Fig. 17*

It is important that:
    (i)    Begin forwards, step strongly forwards foot pointing IN THE DIRECTION of the action.
    (ii)   Chest down to knee of bent leg.
    (iii)  Hands at right angles to line of action.

*Fig. 17(a)*

    (iv)   Push hard from the bent leg and swing the other up — wide straddle of legs.
    (v)   Arms straight.
    (vi)  Eyes looking downwards.

*Fig. 18*

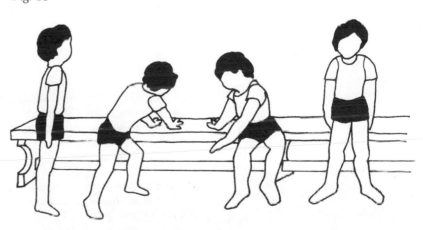

The teaching stages are:

(a)  The child stands at one end of a bench with his left side towards it as in *Fig. 18*. He steps forward on to this left foot, placing his left hand on the bench followed by the right hand. As his right foot comes to the floor, followed by his left he will turn to end up with his back to the bench.

(b)  The pupil tries to get his foot higher in performing the cartwheel. The teacher will have to support many children at this stage.

(c)  The whole should now be attempted on mats, or along a straight line on the floor.

**8 Round Off**   The finished action should look like the drawings in *Fig. 19*.

*Fig. 19*

The round-off differs from the cartwheel as follows:

(i)   It is generally performed with more speed and often finishes with a jump from 2 feet.

(ii)  There are two quarter turns of the body and the direction therefore changes from initial *forward* movement to final *backward* position.

(iii) It would normally begin with a hurdle step (see jumping).

*Note*:  The hand placings are crucial to the successful turning within the action. The legs snap together at the top of the action.

*Teaching*
Stages can be:

(i)   Cartwheel

(ii)  Handstand/snap down

(iii) Lunge step to round-off (*i.e.* not hurdle step approach)

(iv)  Standing hurdle step to round-off

(v)   1–2 steps into hurdle step to round off

# PHYSIOLOGICAL GUIDE

There are three main physiological aspects of gymnastics, namely Joint Mobility sometimes referred to a suppleness or flexibility, Muscle Strength and Stamina. Stamina to some extent can be left to be achieved in other aspects of physical education but strength and mobility cannot be left to chance and it is perhaps mainly through gymnastics that children gain in all round strength and mobility. Certainly each lesson should have a warm up and body preparation section. The aim of the warm up is self evident, to literally warm up the body, whilst the body preparation section is a developmental process.

**Mobility**
This means making the joints move through their full range of movement. In every day life our joints or rather our muscles which control our joints become habituated to our normal tasks and when we are required to do something out of the normal routine we find it difficult or even impossible to achieve.

By getting into the habit of 'stretching' our joints regularly we maintain normal range of movement. Many gymnastic activities put children into positions they would not normally find themselves in. Certain skills cannot be *safely* attempted or performed without the requisite degree of joint mobility.

All mobility exercises should be done *slowly* making the joint go the limits (just after it begins to hurt a bit) by active use of the muscles. If these movements are done quickly an automatic reflex stops the joint from getting anywhere near its full range because at speed the joint could be damaged.

Where possible the joint should be stretched as far as possible and then the child tries to do a further 3 little presses in this fully stretched or end position.

175

All the major joint complexes should receive attention systematically.

### Strength

Strength can only be increased by making the muscles work harder than they do normally. In other words they must be 'overloaded'. This can be done either by increasing the load or making the muscles do many more repetitions.

In gymnastics body weight is used to overload the muscles there is no need for weights. For example: (i) Stand 3 feet from a wall and push yourself from the wall to a standing position. (ii) Prone position (press up position) hands on bench. Push up from bench. (iii) Press up on floor. (iv) Press up in handstand.

This is progressively more difficult as more and more body weight is thrust upon the upper arms. An example of overload by repetition is squat thrusts which you will all have seen on 'Super Stars'.

- (i)   How many can each member of the class do in 15 secs.
- (ii)  Next lesson try to beat your own record in 15 secs.
- (iii) When everyone has achieved say 5 more in 15 secs. then lengthen the time to 20 secs. and repeat (a) and (b).

This strengthens, increases power and increases local muscle endurance (stamina).

Push strength, jump strength, trunk bending, stretching and arching strength are essential in gymnastics.